An
AUTOBIOGRAPHY
of

DAVY CROCKETT

Skyhorse Publishing books may be purchased in bulk at special discounts for sales promotion, corporate gifts, fund-raising, or educational purposes. Special editions can also be created to specifications. For details, contact the Special Sales Department, Skyhorse Publishing, 307 West 36th Street, 11th Floor, New York, NY 10018 or info@skyhorsepublishing.com.

Skyhorse® and Skyhorse Publishing® are registered trademarks of Skyhorse Publishing, Inc.®, a Delaware corporation.

Visit our website at www.skyhorsepublishing.com.

10 9 8 7 6 5 4 3 2 1

Library of Congress Cataloging-in-Publication Data is available on file.

Cover design by Jane Sheppard

Print ISBN: 978-1-63220-484-4
Ebook ISBN: 978-1-62873-176-7

Printed in the United States of America

An
AUTOBIOGRAPHY
of
DAVY CROCKETT

Edited by Stephen Brennan

SKYHORSE PUBLISHING

For Andy, remembering all those days in the woods when we both really believed we were Davy Crockett.

Contents

Introduction

Not much you can say about Davy Crockett hasn't already been said. Or is there? We all know Davy Crockett, or think we do—though we frequently mix the man and the myth together. But the history of the man is pretty straight up. There are records and reports of all kinds: land deeds, commercial undertakings and other legal documents, newspaper citations, campaign circulars and election records, all attesting to the when's and where's of Crockett's life. There are memoirs and reminiscences, by friend and by foe. There are a hundred personal anecdotes by men who actually shook his hand, and thousands more by folks who—whatever they might claim—never had that privilege. And best of all, we have this wonderful work, the true story of the man, in his own words. It is a rare thing to have the actual words—sworn and attested to—of a Mythic Hero, for certainly that is just what David Crockett has become.

This idea of mythic hero is not so easily unpacked, but we can get something of a make on it by having a look at the journey or process by which David Crockett of Tennessee became Davy Crockett, King of the Wild Frontier. David appears first, in history and in lore, as a local hero, an honest man, a doer of mighty deeds, and beloved by his neighbors. They soon make him a Justice of the Peace, elect him Colonel of a local militia regiment, and later to the Tennessee State Legislature. When in 1827, he is elected to Congress, he becomes, almost over-night, a national celebrity and a veritable legend in his own time. Here was your bone fide wild man, come out of the frontier West—a backwoods firecracker, a *Gentleman from the Cane*, an honest man, independent, self-reliant, funny as a cow up a tree. His unlettered charm, outsized personality, and his deep humor must have been striking, but something else was at work here. At that time the young nation was settling on an idea of itself, and part of that process was a general recognition of, or choice of a national icon or type. Just as fifty years later the *Cowboy* was to play the role, at that time it was the *Frontiersman* who most engaged the popular imagination. Here was the new man, the real man—an altogether better man, come out of the West, and Davy Crockett was his avatar.

In Washington, Crockett stood up against Andrew Jackson's very popular government, and was finally driven from office. And then, like magic, and like many another legendary hero, Crockett disappeared. Now you see him, now you don't. Months later the world wondered to hear of his fiery death at the Alamo. There began the myth. Because the action or force of myth is implosive, over time, meanings gather to it, significances adhere, and each subsequent age latches-on to some aspect of the story that best resonates with its own challenging time. In this sense, each era remakes the myth of Davy Crockett in its own image.

But, hold on a jiff—before we get carried away—we do have here, between these very covers, the actual words of the man himself.

The text of this version of Davy's Autobiography is composed of two works, originally published just over a year apart: *A Narrative of the Life of David Crockett of the State of Tennessee—Written by*

Himself (and his friend Thomas Chilton, Representative from the State of Kentucky) and *An Account of Colonel Crockett's Tour to the North and Down East, etc.—Written by Himself* (and Representative William Clark, from the Commonwealth of Pennsylvania.) It appears that Crockett took a larger hand in the writing of the first publication. Tom Chilton and he had both originally come to Washington as western Democrats, pledged Jackson men, devoted to the cause of the *Common Man*. Both men seem to have soured on Jackson, his machine and his new Age or order, at about the same time. Both men bunked in the same DC boardinghouse. One can imagine the late nights in an upstairs room. The whale-oil lamp flickers. We see Tom, hunched over the table scribbling away, while Davy stalks the floor, forever talking and remembering and laughing. Good chance there's a bottle in his hand. The friendship of the two men appears evident in their collaboration, a near perfect partnership between an author and his ghost.

With William Clark and the second book it was different. *An Account of Colonel Crockett's Tour, etc.* was complied from notes Crockett provided Clark and is much less a masterpiece, and much more a campaign document, written with an eye to cashing in on his notoriety. Even with all the care Clark takes render it in a backwoods idiom, this book is little more than travelogue with sketches and a few tall tales of bear-hunting adventures.

But Crockett approved the finished version and put his name to it, so we have to count it as his. Ultimately, there's no way to definitively fix the relative contributions between Crockett, Chilton and Clark—we have to take them all in all. Our choice for inclusion in a true autobiography must fall only on those works that David actually set his hand to, and acknowledged as his own. Of all the dozens of versions of his story making that claim, all the penny-dreadful romances, the almanacs, stage-plays, movies, and TV shows, only these two books can fairly be counted as Davy Crockett's Autobiography.

In publishing ergot, these two volumes were originally both "crashed"—that is, hurried into print. These first publications were without any decoration, while our version is lavishly illustrated with drawings, wood-block prints, lithographs, cartoons, and por-traiture—all early to mid-nineteenth century works. They are un-captioned and un-attributed, in black and white, and embedded throughout. The aim is to give our rendering of Crockett's story a visual dimension, roughly consistent with the iconography of his own time. The chapter headings are mine own.

Stephen Brennan

West Cornwall, CT, 2011

Preface

Fashion is a thing I care mighty little about, except when it happens to run just exactly according to my own notion; and I was mighty nigh sending out my book without any preface at all until a notion struck me that perhaps it was necessary to explain a little the reason why and wherefore I had written it.

Most authors seek fame, but I seek for justice,—a holier impulse than ever entered into the ambitious struggles of the votaries of that *fickle, flirting* goddess.

A publication has been made to the world, which has done me much injustice; and the catchpenny errors which it contains, have been already too long sanctioned by my silence. I don't know the author of the book—and indeed I don't want to know him; for after he has taken such a liberty with my name and made such an effort to hold me up to public ridicule, he cannot calculate on any thing but my displeasure. If he had been content to have written his opinions about me, however contemptuous they might have been, I should have had less reason to complain. But when he professes to give my narrative, (as he often does), in my own language, and then puts into my mouth such language as would disgrace even an outlandish African, he must himself be sensible of the injustice he has done me, and the trick he has played off on the public. I have met with hundreds, if not with thousands of people who have formed their opinions of my appearance, habits, language, and every thing else from that deceptive work.

They have almost in every instance expressed the most profound astonishment at finding me in human shape, and with the *countenance, appearance*, and *common feelings* of a human being. It is to correct all these false notions and to do justice to myself that I have written.

It is certain that the writer of the book alluded to has gathered up many imperfect scraps of information concerning me, as in parts of his work there is some little semblance of truth. But I ask him, if this notice should ever reach his eye, how would he have liked it if I had treated him so? If I had put together such a bundle of ridiculous stuff and headed it with his name and sent it out upon the world without ever even condescending to ask *his* permission? To these questions, all upright men must give the same answer. It was wrong; and the desire to make money by it is no apology for such injustice to a fellow man.

But I let him pass; as my wish is greatly more to vindicate myself than to condemn him.

In the following pages I have endeavoured to give the reader a plain, honest, homespun account of my state in life, and some few of the difficulties which have attended me along its journey, down to this time. I am perfectly aware that I have related many small and, as I fear, uninteresting circumstances; but if so, my apology is that it was rendered necessary by a desire to link the different periods of my life together as they have passed, from my childhood onward, and thereby to enable the reader to select such parts of it as he may relish most, if indeed there is any thing in it which may suit his palate.

I have also been operated on by another consideration. It is this: I know that obscure as I am, my name is making a considerable deal of fuss in the world. I can't tell why it is, nor to what end. Go where I will, everybody seems anxious to get a peep at me and it would be hard to tell which would have the advantage, if I, the

"Government" and "Black Hawk," and a great eternal big caravan of *wild varments* were all to be showed at the same time in four different parts of any of the big cities in the nation. I am not so sure that I shouldn't get the most custom of any of the crew. There must therefore be something in me, or about me, that attracts attention, which is even mysterious to myself. I can't understand it and I therefore put all the facts down, leaving the reader free to take his choice of them.

On the subject of my style, it is bad enough, in all conscience, to please critics, if that is what they are after. They are a sort of vermin, though, that I sha'n't even so much as stop to brush off. If they want to work on my book, just let them go ahead; and after they are done, they had better blot out all their criticisms, than to know what opinion I would express of them and by what sort of a curious name I would call them, if i was standing near them and looking over their shoulders. They will, at most, have only their trouble for their pay. But I rather expect I shall have them on my side.

But I don't know of any thing in my book to be criticised on by honourable men. Is it on my spelling? That's not my trade. Is it on my grammar? I hadn't time to learn it and make no pretensions to it. Is it on the order and arrangement of my book? I never wrote one before and never read very many; and, of course, know mighty little about that. Will it be on the authorship of the book? This I claim and I'll hang on to it, like a wax plaster. The whole book is my own and every sentiment and sentence in it. I would not be such a fool, or knave either, as to deny that I have had it hastily run over by a friend or so and that some little alterations have been made in the spelling and grammar; and I am not so sure that it is not the worse of even that, for I despise this way of spelling contrary to nature. And as for grammar, it's pretty much a thing of nothing at last, after all the fuss that's made about it. In some places, I wouldn't suffer either the spelling or grammar or any thing else to be touched and therefore it will be found in my own way.

But if any body complains that I have had it looked over, I can only say to him, her, or them, as the case may be, that while critics were learning grammar and learning to spell, I, and "Doctor Jackson, L.L.D." were fighting in the wars; and if our books and messages and proclamations and cabinet writings and so forth and so on, should need a little looking over, and a little correcting of the spelling and the grammar to make them it for use, its just nobody's business. Big men have more important matters to attend to than crossing their *t*'s, and dotting their *i*'s, and such like smal things. But the "Government's" name is to the proclamation, and my name is to the book; and if I didn't write the book, the "Government" didn't write the proclamation, which no man *dares to deny!*

But just read for yourself, and my ears for a heel tap, if before you get through you don't say, with many a good-natured smile and hearty laugh, "This is truly the very thing itself—the exact image of its Author."

DAVID CROCKETT

WASHINGTON CITY,
February 1st, 1834.

PART ONE

A Narrative of the Life of David Crockett to the State of Tennessee

A

NARRATIVE

OF THE

LIFE OF DAVID CROCKETT,

TO THE

STATE OF TENNESEE.

I leave this rule for others when I'm dead,
Be always sure you're right—THEN GO AHEAD!
THE AUTHOR.

WRITTEN BY HIMSELF.

SIXTH EDITION.

PHILADELPHIA.
E. L. CAREY AND A. HART.
BALTIMORE:
CAREY, HART & CO.

1834.

As the public seem to feel some interest in the history of an individual so humble as I am, and as that history can be so well known to no person living as to myself, I have, after so long a time, and under many pressing solicitations from my friends and acquaintances, at last determined to put my own hand to it and lay before the world a narrative on which they may at least rely as being true. And seeking no ornament or colouring for a plain, simple tale of truth, I throw aside all hypocritical and fawning apologies and, according to my own maxim, just *"go ahead."*

Where I am not known, I might perhaps gain some little credit by having thrown around this volume some of the flowers of learning; but revolutionary war. I personally know nothing about it, for it happened to be a little before my day; but from himself, and many others who were well acquainted with its troubles and afflictions, I have learned that he was a soldier in the revolutionary war, and took part in that bloody struggle. He fought, according to my information, in the battle at Kings Mountain against the British and Tories, and in some other engagements of which my remembrance is too imperfect to enable me to speak with any certainty. At some time, though I cannot say certainly when my father, as I have understood, lived in Lincoln county, in the state of North Carolina. How long, I don't know. But when he removed from there, he settled in that district of country which is now embraced in the east division of Tennessee, though it was not then erected into a state.

He settled there under dangerous circumstances, both to himself and his family, as the country was full of Indians who were, at that time, very troublesome. By the Creeks, my grandfather and grandmother Crockett were both murdered in their own house and on the very spot of ground where Rogersville, in Hawkins county, now stands. At the same time, the Indians wounded Joseph Crockett, a brother to my father, by a ball, which broke his arm; and took James prisoner, who was still a younger brother than Joseph, and who, from natural defects, was less able to make his escape, as he was both deaf and dumb. He remained with them for seventeen years and nine months, when he was discovered and recollected by my father and his eldest brother, William Crockett; and was purchased by them from an Indian trader at a price which I do not now remember. But so it was, that he was delivered up to them, and they returned him to his relatives. He now lives in Cumberland county, in the state of Kentucky, though I have not seen him for many years.

My father and mother had six sons and three daughters. I was the fifth son. What a pity I hadn't been the seventh! For then I might have been, by *common consent,* called *doctor,* as a heap of people get to be great men. But, like many of them, I stood no chance to become great in any other way than by accident. As my father was very poor, and living as he did far back in the back woods, he had neither the means nor the opportunity to give me, or any of the rest of his children, any learning.

But before I get on the subject of my own troubles, and a great many very funny things that have happened to me, like all other historians and bioagraphers, I should not only inform the public that I was born, myself, as well as other folks, but that this important event took place, according to the best information I have received on the subject, on the 17th of August, in the year 1786; whether by day or night, I believe I never heard, but if I did I, have forgotten. I suppose, however, it is not very material to my present purpose, nor to the world, as the more important fact is well attested that I was born; and indeed it might be inferred, from my present size and appearance, that I was pretty *well born,* though I have never yet attached myself to that numerous and worthy society.

At that time my father lived at the mouth of Lime Stone, on the Nola-chucky river; and for the purpose not only of showing what sort of a man I now am, but also to show how soon I began to be a *sort of a little man,* I have endeavoured to take the back track of life, in order to fix on the first thing that I can remember. But even then, as now, so many things were happening, that as Major Jack Downing would say, they are all in "a pretty considerable of a snarl," and I find it "kinder hard" to fix on that thing, among them all, which really happened first. But I think it likely I have hit on the outside line of my recollection; as one thing happened at which I was so badly scared that it seems to me I could not have forgotten it if it had happened a little time only after I was born. Therefore it furnishes me with no certain evidence of my age at the time; but I know one thing very well and that is that when it happened, I had no knowledge of the use of breeches, for I had never had any nor worn any.

But the circumstance was this: My four elder brothers, and a well-grown boy of about fifteen years old by the name of Campbell, and myself, were all playing on the river's side when all the rest of them got into my father's canoe and put out to amuse themselves on the water, leaving me on the shore alone.

Just a little distance below them, there was a fall in the river, which went slap-right straight down. My brothers, though they were little fellows, had been used to paddling the canoe and could have carried it safely anywhere about there; but this fellow Campbell wouldn't let them have the paddle, but, fool like, undertook to manage it himself. I reckon he had never seen a water craft before and it went just any way but the way he wanted it. There he paddled and paddled and paddled, all the while going wrong, until, in a short time, here they were all going, straight forward, stern foremost, right plump to the falls; and if they had only had a fair shake, they would have gone over as slick as a whistle. It wasn't this, though, that seared me; for I was so infernal mad that they had left me on the shore that I had as soon have seen them all go over the falls a bit, as any other way. But their danger was seen by a man by the name of Kendall, but I'll be shot if it was Amos; for I believe I would know him if I was to see him. This man Kendall was working in a field on the bank and knowing there was no time to lose, he started full tilt, and here he come like a cane brake afire and as he ran, he threw off his coat, and then his jacket, and then his shirt, for I know when he got to the water he had nothing on but his breeches. But seeing him in such a hurry, and tearing off his clothes as he went, I had no doubt but that the devil or something else was after him, and close on him, too, as he was running within an inch of his life. This alarmed me and I screamed out like a young painter. But Kendall didn't stop for this. He went ahead with all might, and as full bent on saving the boys, as Amos was on moving the deposits. When he came to the water he plunged in, and where it was too deep to wade he would swim, and where it was shallow enough he went bolting on; and by such exertion as I never saw at any other time in my life, he reached the canoe, when it was within twenty or thirty feet of the falls; and so great was the suck and so swift the current, that poor Kendall had a hard time of it to stop them at last, as Amos will to stop the mouths of the people about his stockjobbing. But he hung on to the canoe, till he got it stop'd, and then draw'd it out of danger. When they got out, I found the boys were more scared than I had been, and the only thing that comforted me was the belief that it was a punishment on them for leaving me on shore.

Shortly after this, my father removed and settled in the same county about ten miles above Greenville.

Then another circumstance happened which made a lasting impression on my memory, though I was but a small child. Joseph Hawkins, who was a brother to my mother, was in the woods hunting for deer. He was passing near a thicket of brush in which one of our neighbours was gathering some grapes, as it was in the fall of the year and the grape season. The body of the man was hid by the brush and it was only as he would raise his hand to pull the bunches that any part of him could be seen. It was a likely place for deer and my uncle, having no suspicion that it was any human being, but supposing the raising of the hand to be the occasional twitch of a deer's ear, fired at the lump and, as the devil would have it, unfortunately shot the man through the body. I saw my father draw a silk handkerchief through the bullet hole, and entirely through his body; yet after a while he got well, as little as any one would have thought it. What become of him, or whether he is dead or alive, I don't know; but I reckon he did'ent fancy the business of gathering grapes in an out-of-the-way thicket soon again.

The next move my father made was to the mouth of Cove creek where he and a man by the name of Thomas Galbreath undertook to build a mill in partnership. They went on very well with their work until it was nigh done, when there came the second epistle to Noah's fresh and away went their mill, shot, lock, and barrel. I remember the water rose so high, that it got up into the house we lived in and my father moved us out of it to keep us from being drowned. I was now about seven or eight years old, and have a pretty distinct recollection of every thing that was going on. From his bad luck in that business, and being ready to wash out from mill building, my father again removed and this time settled in

Jefferson county, now in the state of Tennessee; where he opened a tavern on the road from Abbingdon to Knoxville.

His tavern was on a small scale, as he was poor, and the principal accommodations which he kept were for the waggoners who travelled the road. Here I remained with him until I was twelve years old and about that time, you may guess, if you belong to Yankee land, or reckon if, like me, you belong to the back-woods, that I began to make up my acquaintance with hard times and a plenty of them.

An old Dutchman by the name of Jacob Siler, who was moving from Knox county to Rockbridge, in the state of Virginia, in passing, made a stop at my father's house. He had a large stock of cattle that he was carrying on with him and I suppose made some proposition to my father to hire someone to assist him.

Being hard run every way and having no thought, as I believe, that I was cut out for a Congressman or the like, young as I was, and as little as I knew about travelling or being from home, he hired me to the old Dutchman to go four hundred miles on foot with a perfect stranger that I never had seen until the evening before. I set out with a heavy heart, it is true, but I went ahead until we arrived at the place which was three miles from what is called the Natural Bridge, and made a stop at the house of a Mr. Hartley, who was father-in-law to Mr. Siler, who had hired me. My Dutch master was very kind to me and he gave me five or six dollars, being pleased, as he said, with my services.

This, however, I think was a bait for me, as he persuaded me to stay with him and not return any more to my father. I had been taught so many lessons of obedience by my father that I at first supposed I was bound to obey this man, or at least I was afraid openly to disobey him; and I therefore stayed with him and tried to put on a look of perfect contentment until I got the family all to believe I was fully satisfied. I had been there about four or five weeks when one day myself and two other boys were playing on the roadside some distance from the house. There came along three waggons. One belonged to an old man by the name of Dunn and the others to two of his sons. They had each of them a good team, and were all bound for Knoxville. They had been in the habit of stopping at my father's as they passed the road and I made myself known to the old gentleman and informed him of my situation. I expressed a wish to get back to my father and mother, if they could fix any plan for me to do so. They told me that they would stay that night at a tavern seven miles from there, and that if I could get to them before day the next morning they would take me home. This was a Sunday evening. I went back to the good old Dutchman's house and, as good fortune would have it, he and the family get out on a visit. I gathered my clothes and whatever money I had and put them all together under the head of my bed. I went to bed early that night, but sleep seemed to be a stranger to me. For though I was a wild boy, I dearly loved my father and mother and their images appeared to be so deeply fixed in my mind that I could not sleep for thinking of them. And then the fear that when I should attempt to go out and be discovered and called to a halt, filled me with anxiety. Between my childish love of home, on the one hand, and the fears of which I have spoken, on the other, I felt mighty queer.

But so it was, about three hours before day in the morning I got up to make my start. When I got out, I found it was snowing fast and that the snow was then on the ground about eight inches deep. I had not even the advantage of moonlight and the whole sky was hid by the falling snow so that I had to guess at my way to the big road which was about a half mile from the house. I however pushed ahead and soon got to it, and then pursued it, in the direction to the waggons.

I could not have pursued the road if I had not guided myself by the opening it made between the timber, as the snow was too deep to leave any part of it to be known by either seeing or feeling.

Before I overtook the waggons, the earth was covered about as deep as my knees and my tracks filled so briskly after me, that by daylight, my Dutch master could have seen no trace which I left.

I got to the place about an hour before day. I found the waggoners already stirring and engaged in feeding and preparing their horses for a start. Mr. Dunn took me in and treated me with great kindness. My heart was more deeply impressed by meeting with such a friend and at such a time than by wading the snow-storm by night, or all the other sufferings which my mind had endured. I warmed myself by the fire, for I was very cold, and after an early breakfast, we set out on our journey. The thoughts of home now began to take the entire possession of my mind and I almost numbered the sluggish turns of the wheels, and much more certainly the miles of our travel, which appeared to me to count mighty slow. I continued with my kind protectors until we got to the house of a Mr. John Cole on Roanoke, when my impatience became so great that I determined to set out on foot and go ahead by myself, as I could travel twice as fast in that way as the waggons could.

Mr. Dunn seemed very sorry to part with me and used many arguments to prevent me from leaving him. But home, poor as it was, again rushed on my memory and it seemed ten times as dear to me as it ever had before. The reason was that my parents were there and all that I had been accustomed to in the hours of childhood and infancy was there; and there my anxious little heart panted also to be. We remained at Mr. Coles that night, and early in the morning I felt that I couldn't stay; so, taking leave of my friends the waggoners, I went forward on foot, until I was fortunately overtaken by a gentleman who was returning from market, to which he had been with a drove of horses. He had a led horse, with a bridle and saddle on him and he kindly offered to let me get on his horse and ride him. I did so, and was glad of the chance, for I was tired, and was, moreover, near the first crossing of Roanoke, which I would have been compelled to wade, cold as the water was, if I had not fortunately met this good man. I travelled with him in this way without any thing turning up worth recording, until we got within fifteen miles of my father's house. There we parted, and he went on to Kentucky and I trudged on homeward, which I reached that evening. The name of this kind gentleman I have entirely forgotten and I am sorry for it, for it deserves a high place in my little book. A remembrance of his kindness to a little straggling boy, and a stranger to him, has however a resting place in my heart, and there it will remain as long as I live.

* * *

HAVING gotten home, as I have just related, I remained with my father until the next fall, at which time he took it into his head to send me to a little country school which was kept in the neighbourhood by a man whose name was Benjamin Kitchen; though I believe he was no way connected with the cabinet. I went four days and had just began to learn my letters a little when I had an unfortunate falling out with one of the scholars, a boy much larger and older than myself. I knew well enough that though the school-house might do for a still hunt, it wouldn't do for *a drive,* and so I concluded to wait until I could get him out, and then I was de-termined to give him salt and vinegar. I waited till in the evening, when the larger scholars were spelling, I slip'd out and, going some distance along his road, I lay by the way-side in the bushes waiting for him to come along. After a while he and his company came on sure enough and I pitched out from the bushes and set on him like a wild cat. I scratched his face all to a flitter jig and soon made him cry out for quarters in good earnest. The fight being over, I went on home and the next morning started again to school; but do you think I went? No, indeed. I was very clear of it; for I expected the master would lick me up, as bad as I had the boy. So, instead of going to the school-house, I laid out in the woods all day until in the evening the scholars were dismissed, and my brothers, who were also going to school, came along, returning home. I wanted to conceal this whole business from my father, and I therefore persuaded them not to tell on me, which they agreed to.

Things went on in this way for several days; I starting with them to school in the morning and returning with them in the evening, but lying out in the woods all day. At last, however, the master wrote a note to my father, inquiring why I was not sent to school. When he read this note, he called me up, and I knew very well that I was in a devil of a hobble, for my father had been taking a few *horns,* and was in a good condition to make the fur fly. He called on me to know why I had not been at school? I told him I was afraid to go and that the master would whip me; for I knew quite well if I was turned over to this old Kitchen, I should be cooked up to a cracklin in little or no time. But I soon found that I was not to expect a much better fate at home; for my father told me, in a very angry manner, that he would whip me an eternal sight worse than the master if I didn't start immediately to the school. I tried again to beg off but nothing would do but to go to the school. Finding me rather too slow about starting, he gathered about a two year old hickory and broke after me. I put out with all my might and soon we were both up to the top of our speed. We had a tolerable tough race for about a mile; but mind me, not on the school-house road, for I was trying to get as far the t'other way as possible. And I yet believe if my father and the schoolmaster could both have levied on me about that time, I should never have been called on to sit in the councils of the nation, for I think they would have used me up. But fortunately for me, about this time, I saw just before me a hill over which I made headway like a young steamboat. As soon as I had passed over it, I turned to one side and hid myself in the bushes.

Here I waited until the old gentleman passed by, puffing and blowing, as tho' his steam was high enough to burst his boilers. I waited until he gave up the hunt and passed back again. I then cut out and went to the house of an acquaintance who was just about to start with a drove. His name was Jesse Cheek, and I hired myself to go with him, determining not to return home, as home and the school-house had both become too hot for me. I had an elder brother, who also hired to go with the same drove. We set out and went on through Abbingdon, and the county seat of Withe county, in the state of Virginia; and then through Lynchburgh, by Orange court-house, and Charlottesville, passing through what was called Chester Gap, on to a town called Front Royal, where my employer sold out his drove to a man by the name of Vanmetre; and I was started homeward again in company with a brother of the first owner of the drove with one horse between us, having left my brother to come on with the balance of the company.

I traveled on with my new comrade about three days journey but much to his discredit, as I then thought and still think, he took care all the time to ride but never to tie. At last I told him to go ahead, and I would come when I got ready. He gave me four dollars to bear my expenses upwards of four hundred miles and then cut out and left me.

I purchased some provisions and went on slowly until at length I fell in with a waggoner with whom I was disposed to scrape up a hasty acquaintance. I inquired where he lived and where he was going and all about his affairs. He informed me that he lived in Greenville, Tennessee, and was on his way to a place called Gerardstown, fifteen miles below Winchester. He also said that after he should make his journey to that place, he would immediately return to Tennessee. His name was Adam Myers and a jolly good fellow he seemed to be. On a little reflection, I determined to turn back and go with him, which I did; and we journeyed on slowly as waggons commonly do, but merrily enough. I often thought of home and, indeed, wished bad enough to be there; but, when I thought of the school-house and Kitchen, my master and the race with my father and the big hickory he carried, and of the fierceness of the storm of wrath that I had left him in, I was afraid to venture back. For I knew my father's nature so well that I was certain his anger would hang on to him like a turkle does to a fisherman's toe and that if I went back in a hurry, he would give me the devil in three or four ways. But I and the waggoner had traveled two days when we met my brother, who, I before stated, I had left behind when the drove was sold out. He persuaded me to go home but I refused. He pressed me hard and brought up a great many mighty strong arguments to induce me to turn back again. He pictured the pleasure of meeting my mother and my sisters, who all loved me dearly, and told me what uneasiness they had already suffered about me. I could not help shedding tears, which I did not often do, and my affections all pointed back to those dearest friends and, as I thought, nearly the only ones I had in the world. But then the promised whipping—that was the thing. It came right slap down on every thought of home; and I finally determined that make or break, hit or miss, I would just hang on to my journey, and go ahead with the waggoner. My brother was much grieved at our parting, but he went his way and so did I. We went on until at last we got to Gerardstown where the waggoner tried to get a back load but could not without going to Alexandria. He engaged to go there and I concluded that I would wait until he returned. I set in to work for a man by the name of John Gray, at twenty-five cents per day. My labour, however, was light, such as ploughing in some small grain, in which I succeeded in pleasing the old man very well. I continued working for him until the waggoner got back and for a good long time afterwards as he continued to run his team back and forward, hauling to and from Baltimore. In the next spring, from the proceeds of my daily labour, small as it was, I was able to get me some decent clothes and concluded I would make a trip with the waggoner to Baltimore and see what sort of a place that was and what sort of folks lived there. I gave him the balance of what money I had for safe keeping, which, as well as I recollect, was about seven dollars. We got on well enough until we came near Ellicott's Mills. Our load consisted of flour in barrels. Here I got into the waggon for the purpose of changing my clothing, not thinking that I was in any danger; but while I was in there we were met by some wheel-barrow men who were working on the road and the horses took a scare and away they went, like they had seen a ghost. They made a sudden wheel around and broke the waggon tongue slap, short off, as a pipe-stem; and snap went both of the axletrees at the same time, and of all devlish flouncing about of flour barrels that ever was seen, I reckon this took the beat. Even a rat would have stood a bad chance in a straight race among them, and not much better in a crooked one; for he would have been in a good way to be ground up as fine as ginger by their rolling over him. But this proved to me that if a fellow is born to be hung, he will never be drowned; and, further, that if he is born for a seat in Congress, even flour barrels can't make a mash of him. All these dangers I escaped unhurt, though, like most of the office-holders of these times, for a while I was afraid to say my soul was my own; for I didn't know how soon I should be knocked into a cocked hat and get my walking papers for another country.

We put our load into another waggon and hauled ours to a workman's shop in Baltimore having delivered the flour and there we intended to remain two or three days, which time was necessary to repair the runaway waggon. While I was there I went, one day down to the wharf and was much delighted to see the big ships and their sails all flying; for I had never seen any such things before and, indeed, I didn't believe there were any such things in all nature. After a short time my curiosity induced me to step aboard of one, where I was met by the captain who asked me if I didn't wish to take a voyage to London? I told him I did, for by this time I had become pretty well weaned from home and I cared but little where I was, or where I went, or what become of me. He said he wanted just such a boy as I was, which I was glad to hear. I told him I would go and get my clothes and go with him. He enquired about my parents, where they lived and all about them. I let him know that they lived in Tennessee, many hundred miles off. We soon agreed about my intended voyage and I went back to my friend, the waggoner, and informed him that I was going to London and wanted my money and my clothes. He refused to let me have either and swore that he would confine me and take me back to Tennessee. I took it to heart very much but he kept so close and constant a watch over me that I found it impossible to escape from him until he had started homeward and made several days journey on the road. He was, during this time, very ill to me and threatened me with his waggon whip on several occasions. At length I resolved to leave him at all hazards and so, before day one morning, I got my clothes out of his waggon and cut out on foot without a farthing of money to bear my expenses. For all other friends having failed, I determined then to throw myself on Providence and see how that would use me. I had gone, however, only a few miles when I came up with another waggoner and such was my situation that I felt more than ever the necessity of endeavouring to find a friend. I therefore concluded I would seek for one in him. He was going westwardly and very kindly enquired of me where I was travelling? My youthful resolution, which had brooked almost every thing else, rather gave way at this enquiry; for it brought the loneliness of my situation, and every thing else that was calculated to oppress me, directly to view. My first answer to his question was in a sprinkle of tears, for if the world had been given to me, I could not, at that moment, have helped crying. As soon as the storm of feeling was over, I told him how I had been treated by the waggoner but a little before, who kept what little money I had, and left me without a copper to buy even a morsel of food.

He became exceedingly angry and swore that he would make the other waggoner give up my money, pronouncing him a scoundrel and many other hard names. I told him I was afraid to see him, for he had threatened me with his waggon whip, and I believed he would injure me. But my new friend was a very large, stout-looking man, and as resolute as a tiger. He bid me not to be afraid, still swearing he would have my money or whip it out of the wretch who had it.

We turned and went back about two miles when we reached the place where he was. I went reluctantly; but I depended on my friend for protection. When we got there, I had but little to say; but approaching the waggoner, my friend said to him,

"You damned rascal, you're treated this boy badly."

"You damn'd rascal, you have treated this boy badly." To which he replied it was my fault. He was then asked if he did not get seven dollars of my money, which he confessed. It was then demanded of him; but he declared most solemnly that he had not that amount in the world; that he had spent my money and intended paying it back to me when we got to Tennessee. I then felt reconciled and persuaded my friend to let him alone and we returned to his waggon, geared up, and started. His name I shall never forget while my memory lasts; it was Henry Myers. He lived in

Pennsylvania and I found him what he professed to be, a faithful friend and a clever fellow.

We traveled together for several days, but at length I concluded to endeavour to make my way homeward and for that purpose set out again on foot, and alone. But one thing I must not omit. The last night I stayed with Mr. Myers was at a place where several other waggoners also stayed. He told them before we parted that I was a poor little straggling boy and how I had been treated and that I was without money, though I had a long journey before me through a land of strangers, where it was not even a wilderness.

They were good enough to contribute a sort of money-purse and presented me with three dollars. On this amount I travelled as far as Montgomery court-house, in the state of Virginia, where it gave out. I set in to work for a man by the name of James Caldwell for a month for five dollars, which was about a shilling a day. When this time was out, I bound myself to a man by the name of Elijah Griffith, by trade a hatter, agreeing to work for him four years. I remained with him about eighteen months when he found himself so involved in debt that he broke up and left the country. For this time I had received nothing and was, of course, left without money and with but very few clothes and them very indifferent ones. I, however, set in again and worked about as I could catch employment until I got a little money and some clothing and once more cut out for home. When I reached New River, at the mouth of a small stream called Little River, the white caps were flying so that I couldn't get any body to attempt to put me across. I argued the case as well as I could but they told me there was great danger of being capsized and drowned if I attempted to cross. I told them if I could get a canoe I would venture, caps or no caps. They tried to persuade me out of it; but finding they could not, they agreed I might take a canoe, and so I did, and put off. I tied my clothes to the rope of the canoe to have them safe whatever might happen. But I found it a mighty ticklish business, I tell you. When I got out fairly on the river, I would have given the world, if it had belonged to me, to have been back on shore. But there was no time to lose now, so I just determined to do the best I could and the devil take the hindmost. I turned the canoe across the waves, I had to turn it nearly up the river, as the wind came from that way, and I went about two miles before I could land. When I struck land, my canoe was about half full of water and I was as wet as a drowned rat. But I was so much rejoiced that I scarcely felt the cold, though my clothes were frozen on me; and in this situation, I had to go above three miles before I could find any house or fire to warm at. I, however, made out to get to one at last and then I thought I would warm the inside a little, as well as the outside, that there might be no grumbling.

So I took "a leetle of the creater," that warmer of the cold, and cooler of the hot, and it made me feel so good that I concluded it was like the negro's rabbit, "good any way." I passed on until I arrived in Sullivan county, in the state of Tennessee, and there I met with my brother who had gone with me when I started from home with the cattle drove.

I stayed with him a few weeks and then went on to my father's, which place I reached late in the evening. Several waggons were there for the night and considerable company about the house. I enquired if I could stay all night for I did not intend to make myself known until I saw whether any of the family would find me out. I was told that I could stay and went in, but had mighty little to say to any body. I had been gone so long and had grown so much that the family did not at first know me. And another, and perhaps a stronger reason was, they had no thought or expectation of me, for they all had long given me up for finally lost.

After a while, we were all called to supper. I went with the rest. We had sat down to the table and begun to eat, when my eldest sister recollected me: she sprang up, ran and seized me around the neck, and exclaimed, "Here is my lost brother."

My feelings at this time it would be vain and foolish for me to attempt to describe. I had often thought I felt before, and I suppose I had, but sure I am, I never had felt as I then did. The joy of my sisters and my mother, and, indeed, of all the family, was such that it humbled me and made me sorry that

I hadn't submitted to a hundred whippings sooner than cause so much affliction as they had suffered on my account. I found the family had never heard a word of me from the time my brother left me. I was now almost *fifteen* years old; and my increased age and size, together with the joy of my father, occasioned by my unexpected return, I was sure would secure me against my long dreaded whipping; and so they did. But it will be a source of astonishment to many, who reflect that I am now a member of the American Congress, the most enlightened body of men in the world, that at so advanced an age, the age of fifteen, I did not know the first letter in the book.

I HAD remained for some short time at home with my father when he informed me that he owed a man, whose name was Abraham Wilson, the sum of thirty-six dollars and that if I would set in and work out the note, so as to lift it for him, he would discharge me from his service and I might go free. I agreed to do this, and went immediately to the man who held my father's note and contracted with him to work six months for it. I set in and worked with all my might, not losing a single day in the six months. When my time was out, I got my father's note and then declined working with the man any longer, though he wanted to hire me mighty bad. The reason was, it was a place where a heap of bad company met to drink and gamble and I wanted to get away from them, for I know'd very well if I stayed there, I should get a bad name, as nobody could be respectable that would live there. I therefore returned to my father, and gave him up his paper, which seemed to please him mightily, for though he was poor, he was an honest man, and always tried mighty hard to pay off his debts.

I next went to the house of an honest old Quaker by the name of John Kennedy, who had removed from North Carolina, and proposed to hire myself to him at two shillings a day. He agreed to take me a week on trial at the end of which he appeared pleased with my work and informed me that he held a note on my father for forty dollars and that he would give me that note if I would work for him six months. I was certain enough that I should never get any part of the note; but then I remembered it was my father that owed it and I concluded it was my duty as a child to help him along and ease his lot as much as I could. I told the Quaker I would take him up at his offer and immediately went to work. I never visited my father's house during the whole time of this engagement, though he lived only fifteen miles off. But when it was finished, and I had got the note, I borrowed one of my employer's horses, and, on a Sunday evening, went to pay my parents a visit. Some time after I got there, I pulled out the note and handed it to my father, who supposed Mr. Kennedy had sent it for collection. The old man looked mighty sorry and said to me he had not the money to pay it, and didn't know what he should do. I then told him I had paid it for him and it was then his own that it was not presented for collection, but as a present from me. At this, he shed a heap of tears and as soon as he got a little over it, he said he was sorry he couldn't give me any thing, he was too poor.

The next day, I went back to my old friend, the Quaker, and set in to work for him for some clothes; for I had now worked a year without getting any money at all, and my clothes were nearly all worn out and what few I had left were mighty indifferent. I worked in this way for about two months; and in that time a young woman from North Carolina, who was the Quaker's niece, came on a visit to his house. And now I am just getting on a part of my history that I know I never can forget. For though I have heard people talk about hard loving, yet I reckon no poor devil in this world was ever cursed with such hard love as mine has always been, when it came on me. I soon found myself head over heels in love with this girl, whose name the public could make no use of. I thought that if all the hills about there were pure chink, and all belonged to me, I would give them if I could just talk to her as I wanted to; but I was afraid to begin, for when I would think of saying any thing to her, my heart would begin to flutter like a duck in a puddle; and if I tried to outdo it and speak, it would get right smack up in my throat, and choak me like a cold potatoe. It bore on my mind in this way, till at last I concluded I must die if I didn't broach the subject; and so I determined to begin and hang on a trying to speak, till my heart would get out of my throat one way or t'other. And so one day at it I went and after several trials I could say a little. I told her how well I loved her; that she was the darling object of my soul and body; and I must have her or else I should pine down to nothing, and just die away with the consumption.

I found my talk was not disagreeable to her but she was an honest girl and didn't want to deceive nobody. She told me she was engaged to her cousin, a son of the old Quaker. This news was worse to me than war, pestilence, or famine; but still I knowed I could not help myself. I saw quick enough my cake was dough and I tried to cool off as fast as possible; but I had hardly safety pipes enough, as my love was so hot as mighty nigh to burst my boilers. But I didn't press my claims any more, seeing there was no chance to do any thing.

I began now to think that all my misfortunes growed out of my want of learning. I had never been to school but four days, as the reader has already seen, and did not yet know a letter.

I thought I would try to go to school some; and as the Quaker had a married son, who was living about a mile and a half from him, and keeping a school, I proposed to him that I would go to school four days in the week, and work for him the other two, to pay my board and schooling. He agreed I might come on those terms and so at it I went, learning and working back and forwards, until I had been with him nigh on to six months. In this time I learned to read a little in my primer, to write my own name, and to cypher some in the three first rules in figures. And this was all the schooling I ever had in my life, up to this day. I should have continued longer, if it hadn't been that I concluded I couldn't do any longer without a wife; and so I cut out to hunt me one.

I found a family of very pretty little girls that I had known when very young. They had lived in the same neighborhood with me and I had thought very well of them. I made an offer to one of them, whose name is nobody's business, no more than the Quaker girl's was, and I found she took it very well. I still continued paying my respects to her, until I got to love her as bad as I had the Quaker's niece; and I would have agreed to fight a whole regiment of wild cats if she would only have said she would have me. Several months passed in this way, during all of which time she continued very kind and friendly. At last, the son of the old Quaker and my first girl had concluded to bring their matter to a close, and my little queen and myself were called on to wait on them. We went on the day and performed our duty as attendants. This made me worse than ever and after it was over, I pressed my claim very hard on her, but she would still give me a sort of an evasive answer.

However, I gave her mighty little peace till she told me at last she would have me. I thought this was glorification enough, even without spectacles. I was then about eighteen years old. We fixed the time to be married and I thought if that day come, I should be the happiest man in the created world, or in the moon, or any where else.

I had by this time got to be mighty fond of the rifle and had bought a capital one. I most generally carried her with me wherever I went, and though I had got back to the old Quaker's to live, who was a very particular man, I would sometimes slip out and attend the shooting matches, where they shot for beef; I always tried, though, to keep it a secret from him. He had at the same time a bound boy living with him who I had gotten into almost as great a notion of the girls as myself. He was about my own age and was deeply smitten with the sister to my intended wife. I know'd it was in vain to try to get the leave of the old man for my young associate to go with me on any of my courting frolics but I thought I could fix a plan to have him along which would not injure the Quaker, as we had no notion that he should ever know it. We commonly slept up-stairs, and at the gable end of the house there was a window. So one Sunday, when the old man and his family were all gone to meeting, we went out and cut a long pole, and, taking it to the house, we set it up on end in the corner, reaching up the chimney as high as the window. After this we would go upstairs to bed and then, putting on our Sunday clothes, would go out at the window, and climb down the pole, take a horse apiece and ride about ten miles to where his sweetheart lived and to the girl I claimed as my wife. I was always mighty careful to be back before day so as to escape being found out and in this way I continued my attentions very closely until a few days before I was to be married, or at least thought I was, for I had no fear that any thing was about to go wrong.

Just now I heard of a shooting-match in the neighbourhood, right between where I lived and my girl's house; and I determined to kill two birds with one stone, to go to the shooting match first, and then to see her. I therefore made the Quaker believe I was going to hunt for deer, as they were pretty plenty about in those parts; but, instead of hunting them, I went straight on to the shooting-match, where I joined in with a partner and we put in several shots for the beef. I was mighty lucky and when the match was over I had won the whole beef. This was on a Saturday and my success had put me in the finest humour in the world. So I sold my part of the beef for five dollars in the real grit, for I believe that was before bank-notes were invented; at least, I had never heard of any. I now started on to ask for my wife for, though the next Thursday was our wedding day, I had never said a word to her parents about it. I had always dreaded the undertaking so bad that I had put the evil hour off and, it seemed to me, that it was more than any human creature could endure. It struck me perfectly speechless for some time and made me feel so weak that I thought I should sink down. I however recovered from my shock after a little and rose and started without any ceremony, or even bidding any body good-bye. The young woman followed me out to the gate and entreated me to go on to her father's and said she would go with me. She said the young man, who was going to marry her sister, had got his license and had asked for her, but she assured me her father and mother both preferred me to him and that she had no doubt but that, if I would go on, I could break off the match. But I found I could go no further. My heart was bruised and my spirits broken down; so I bid her farewell and turned my lonesome and miserable steps back again homeward, concluding that I was only born for hardships, misery, and disappointment. I now began to think that in making me, it was entirely forgotten to make my mate; that I was born odd and should always remain so and that nobody would have me.

But all these reflections did not satisfy my mind, for I had no peace day nor night for several.

"The young woman followed me out to the gate, and entreated me to go on to her father's," &c.

* * *

I CONTINUED in this down-spirited situation for a good long time, until one day I took my rifle and started a hunting. While out, I made a call at the house of a Dutch widow, who had a daughter that was well enough as to smartness, but she was as ugly as a stone fence. She was, however, quite talkative and soon begun to laugh at me about my disappointment.

She seemed disposed, though, to comfort me as much as she could and, for that purpose, told me to keep in good heart, that "there was as good fish in the sea as had ever been caught out of it." I doubted this very much, but whether or not I was certain that she was not one of them, for she was so homely that it almost give me a pain in the eyes to look at her.

But I couldn't help thinking that she had intended what she had said as a banter for me to court her! The last thing in creation I could have thought of doing. I felt little inclined to talk on the subject, it is true; but, to pass off the time, I told her I thought I was born odd and that no fellow to me could be found. She protested against this and said if I would come to their reaping, which was not far off, she would show me one of the prettiest little girls there I had ever seen. She added that the one who had deceived me was nothing to be compared with her. I didn't believe a word of all this, for I had thought that such a piece of flesh and blood as she was had never been manufactured and never would again. I agreed with her, though, that the little varment had treated me so bad that I ought to forget her and yet I couldn't do it. I concluded the best way to accomplish it was to cut out again and see if I could find any other that would answer me and so I told the Dutch girl I would be at the reaping and would bring as many as I could with me.

I employed my time pretty generally in giving information of it, as far as I could, until the day came and I then offered to work for my old friend, the Quaker, two days, if he would let his bound boy go with me one to the reaping. He refused and reproved me pretty considerable roughly for my proposition and said if he was in my place he wouldn't go, that there would be a great deal of bad company there and that I had been so good a boy, he would be sorry for me to get a bad name. But I knowed my promise to the Dutch girl and I was resolved to fulfil it so I shouldered my rifle and started by myself. When I got to the place, I found a large company of men and women and among them an old Irish woman who had a great deal to say. I soon found out from my Dutch girl that this old lady was the mother of the little girl she had promised me, though I had not yet seen her. She was in an outhouse with some other youngsters and had not yet made her appearance. Her mamma, however, was no way bashful. She came up to me and began to praise my red cheeks and said she had a sweetheart for me. I had no doubt she had been told what I come for and all about it. In the evening I was introduced to her daughter and, I must confess, I was plaguy well pleased with her from the word go. She had a good countenance and was very pretty, and I was full bent on making up an acquaintance with her.

It was not long before the dancing commenced and I asked her to join me in a reel. She very readily consented to do so and after we had finished our dance, I took a seat alongside of her and entered into a talk. I found her very interesting; while I was setting by her, making as good a use of my time as I could. Her mother came to us and, very jocularly, called me her son-in-law. This rather confused me, but I looked on it as a joke of the old lady and tried to turn it off as well as I could. I took care to pay as much attention to her through the evening as I could. I went on the old saying of salting the cow to catch the calf. I soon become so much pleased with this little girl that I began to think the Dutch girl had told me the truth when she said there was still good fish in the sea.

We continued our frolic till near day when we joined in some plays, calculated to amuse youngsters. I had not often spent a more agreeable night. In the morning, however, we all had to part and I found my mind had become much better reconciled than it had been for a long time. I went home to the Quaker's and made a bargain to work with his son for a low-priced horse. He was the first one I had ever owned and I was to work six months for him. I had been engaged very closely five or six weeks when this little girl run in my mind so that I concluded I must go and see her and find out what sort of people they were at home. I mounted my horse and away I went to where she lived and when I got there I found her father a very clever old man and the old woman as talkative as ever. She wanted badly to find out all about me and as I thought to see how I would do for her girl. I had not yet seen her about and I began to feel some anxiety to know where she was.

In a short time, however, my impatience was relieved as she arrived at home from a meeting to which she had been. There was a young man with her, who I soon found was disposed to set up claim to her, as he was so attentive to her that I could hardly get to slip in a word edgeways. I began to think I was barking up the wrong tree again but I was determined to stand up to my rack, fodder or no fodder. And so, to know her mind a little on the subject, I began to talk about starting, as I knowed she would then show some sign, from which I could understand which way the wind blowed. It was then near night and my distance was fifteen miles home. At this my little girl soon began to indicate to the other gentleman that his room would be the better part of his company. At length she left him and came to me and insisted mighty hard that I should not go that evening and, indeed, from all her actions and the attempts she made to get rid of him, I saw that she preferred me all holler. But it wasn't long before I found trouble enough in another quarter. Her mother was deeply enlisted for my rival and I had to fight against her influence as well as his. But the girl herself was the prize I was fighting for and as she welcomed me, I was determined to lay siege to her, let what would happen. I commenced a close courtship, having cornered her from her old beau while he set off, looking on, like a poor man at a country frolic, all the time almost gritting his teeth with pure disappointment. But he didn't dare to attempt any thing more, for now I had gotten a start, and I looked at him every once in a while as fierce as a wild-cat. I stayed with her until Monday morning, and then I put out for home.

It was about two weeks after this that I was sent for to engage in a wolf hunt, where a great number of men were to meet with their dogs and guns, and where the best sort of sport was expected. I went as large as life, but I had to hunt in strange woods and in a part of the country which was very thinly inhabited. While I was out it clouded up and I began to get scared. In a little while I was so much so that I didn't know which way home was nor any thing about it. I set out the way I thought it was, but it turned out with me, as it always does with a lost man, I was wrong and took exactly the contrary direction from the right one. And for the information of young hunters, I will just say, in this place, that whenever a fellow gets bad lost, the way home is just the way he don't think it is. This rule will hit nine times out of ten. I went ahead, though, about six or seven miles, when I found night was coming on fast but at this distressing time I saw a little woman streaking it along through the woods like all wrath, and so I cut on too, for I was determined I wouldn't lose sight of her that night any more. I run on till she saw me and she stopped; for she was as glad to see me as I was to see her, as she was lost as well as me. When I came up to her, who should she be but my little girl that I had been paying my respects to. She had been out hunting her father's horses and had missed her way and had no knowledge where she was or how far it was to any house or what way would take us there. She had been travelling all day and was mighty tired and I would have taken her up and toasted her if it hadn't been that I wanted her just where I could see her all the time, for I thought she looked sweeter than sugar; and by this time I loved her almost well enough to eat her.

At last I came to a path that I know'd must go somewhere and so we followed it till we came to a house at about dark. Here we stayed all night. I set up all night courting and in the morning we parted. She went to her home, from which we were distant about seven miles, and I to mine, which was ten miles off.

I now turned in to work again and it was about four weeks before I went back to see her. I continued to go occasionally, until I had worked long enough to pay for my horse, by putting in my gun with my work to the man I had purchased from; and then I began to count whether I was to be deceived again or not. At our next meeting we set the day for our wedding and I went to my father's and made arrangements for an infair and returned to ask her parents for her. When I got there, the old lady appeared to be mighty wrathy; and when I broached the subject, she looked at me as savagely as a meat axe. The old man appeared quite willing and treated me very clever. But I hadn't been there long before the old woman as good as ordered me out of her house. I thought I would put her in mind of old times and see how that would go with her. I told her she had called me her son-in-law before I had attempted to call her my mother-in-law and I thought she ought to cool off. But her Irish was up too high to do any thing with her, so I quit trying. All I cared for was to have her daughter on my side, which I knowed was the case then; but how soon some other fellow might knock my nose out of joint again, I couldn't tell. I however felt rather insulted at the old lady and I thought I wouldn't get married in her house. And so I told her girl that I would come the next Thursday and bring a horse, bridle, and saddle for her and she must be ready to go. Her mother declared I shouldn't have her; but I know'd I should, if somebody else didn't get her before Thursday. I then started, bidding them good day, and went by the house of a justice of the peace, who lived on the way to my father's, and made a bargain with him to marry me.

When Thursday came, all necessary arrangements were made at my father's to receive my wife and so I took my eldest brother and his wife and another brother and a single sister that I had and two other young men with me, and cut out to her father's house to get her. We went on until we got within two miles of the place, where we met a large company that had heard of the wedding and were waiting. Some of that company went on with my brother and sister and the young man I had picked out to wait on me. When they got there, they found the old lady as wrathy as ever. However the old man filled their bottle and the young men returned in a hurry. I then went on with my company, and when I arrived I never pretended to dismount from my horse but rode up to the door and asked the girl if she was ready. She said she was. I then told her to light on the horse I was leading and she did so. Her father, though, had gone out to the gate and when I started he commenced persuading me to stay and marry there; that he was entirely willing to the match, and that his wife, like most women, had entirely too much tongue; but that I oughtn't to mind her. I told him if she would ask me to stay and marry at her house, I would do so. With that he sent for her, and after they had talked for some time out by themselves, she came to me and looked at me mighty good

and asked my pardon for what she had said and invited me stay. She said it was the first child she had ever had to marry and she couldn't bear to see her go off in that way; that if I would light, she would do the best she could for us. I couldn't stand every thing and so I agreed and we got down and went in. I sent off then for my parson and got married in a short time, for I was afraid to wait long for fear of another defeat. We had as good treatment as could be expected and that night all went on well. The next day we cut out for my father's, where we met a large company of people that had been waiting a day and a night for our arrival. We passed the time quite merrily until the company broke up and having gotten my wife, I thought I was completely made up and needed nothing more in the whole world. But I soon found this was all a mistake, for now having a wife, I wanted every thing else and, worse than all, I had nothing to give for it.

I remained a few days at my father's and then went back to my new father-in-law's where, to my surprise, I found my old Irish mother in the finest humour in the world.

She gave us two likely cows and calves, which, though it was a small marriage-portion, was still better than I had expected and indeed it was about all I ever got. I rented a small farm and cabin and went to work but I had much trouble to find out a plan to get any thing to put in my house. At this time, my good old friend the Quaker came forward to my assistance and gave me an order to a store for fifteen dollars' worth of such things as my little wife might choose. With this, we fixed up pretty grand, as we thought, and allowed to get on very well. My wife had a good wheel and knowed exactly how to use it. She was also a good weaver, as most of the Irish are, whether men or women, and being very industrious with her wheel, she had, in little or no time, a fine web of cloth, ready to make up. She was good at that too and at almost any thing else that a woman could do.

We worked on for some years, renting ground and paying high rent, until I found it wan't the thing it was cracked up to be and that I couldn't make a fortune at it at all. So I concluded to quit it and cut out for some new country. In this time we had two sons and I found I was better at increasing my family than my fortune. It was therefore the more necessary that I should hunt some better place to get along; and as I knowed I would have to move at some time I thought it was better to do it before my family got too large so that I might have less to carry.

The Duck and Elk river country was just beginning to settle, and I determined to try that. I had now one old horse and a couple of two year old colts. They were both broke to the halter and my father-in-law proposed that if I went, he would go with me and take one horse to help me move. So we all fixed up and I packed my two colts with as many of my things as they could bear and away we went across the mountains. We got on well enough and arrived safely in Lincoln county on the head of the Mulberry fork of Elk river. I found this a very rich country and so new that game of different sorts was very plenty. It was here that I began to distinguish myself as a hunter and to lay the foundation for all my future greatness but mighty little did I know of what sort it was going to be. Of deer and smaller game I killed abundance; but the bear had been much hunted in those parts before and were not so plenty as I could have wished. I lived here in the years 1809 and '10, to the best of my recollection, and then I moved to Franklin county and settled on Beans creek, where I remained till after the close of the last war.

CHAPTER 2

With General Jackson's Army /
The Creek Indian War / I Come
Home and Marry Again

I was living ten miles below Winchester when the Creek war commenced and, as military men are making so much fuss in the
world at this time, I must give an account of the part I took in the
defence of the country. If it should make me president, why I can't
help it; such things will sometimes happen; and my pluck is never

"to seek nor decline office."

It is true, I had a little rather not; but yet if the government can't get on without taking another president from Tennessee, to finish the work of "retrenchment and reform," why then, I reckon I must go in for it. But I must begin about the war, and leave the other matter for the people to begin on.

The Creek Indians had commenced their open hostilities by a most bloody butchery at Fort Mimms. There had been no war among us for so long, that but few who were not too old to bear arms, knew anything about the business. I, for one, had often thought about war and had often heard it described and I did verily believe in my own mind that I couldn't fight in that way at all; but after my experience convinced me that this was all a notion. For when I heard of the mischief which was done at the fort, I instantly felt like going and I had none of the dread of dying that I expected to feel. In a few days a general meeting of the militia was called for the purpose of raising volunteers and when the day arrived for that meeting, my wife, who had heard me say I meant to go to the war, began to beg me not to turn out. She said she was a stranger in the parts where we lived, had no connexions living near her, and that she and our little children would be left in a lonesome and unhappy situation if I went away. It was mighty hard to go against such arguments as these but my countrymen had been murdered and I knew that the next thing would be, that the Indians would be scalping the women and children all about there if we didn't put a stop to it. I reasoned the case with her as well as I could and told her that if every man would wait till his wife got willing for him to go to war, there would be no fighting done until we would all be killed in our own houses; that I was as able to go as any man in the world; and that I believed it was a duty I owed to my country. Whether she was satisfied with this reasoning or not, she did not tell me; but seeing I was bent on it, all she did was to cry a little and turn about to her work, The truth is, my dander was up, and nothing but war could bring it right again.

I went to Winchester where the muster was to be, and a great
many people had collected, for there was as much fuss among the
people about the war as there is now about moving the deposites.
When the men were paraded, a lawyer by the name of Jones
addressed us and closed by turning out himself, enquiring at the
same time who among us felt like we could fight Indians? This was
the same Mr. Jones who afterwards served in Congress, from the
state of Tennessee. He informed us he wished to raise a company
and that then the men should meet and elect their own officers.
I believe I was about the second or third man that step'd out; but
on marching up and down the regiment a few times, we found we
had a large company We volunteered for sixty days, as it was supposed our services would not be longer wanted. A day or two after
this we met and elected Mr. Jones our captain and also elected our
other officers. We then received orders to start on the next Monday
week; before which time I had fixed as well as I could to go and my
wife had equip'd me as well as she was able for the camp. The time
arrived and I took a parting farewell of my wife and my little boys,
mounted my horse and set sail to join my company. Expecting to
be gone only a short time, I took no more clothing with me than I
supposed would be necessary so that if I got into an Indian battle,
I might not be pestered with any unnecessary plunder to prevent
my having a fair shake with them. We all met and went ahead till
we passed Huntsville and camped at a large spring called Beaty's
spring. Here we stayed for several days in which time the troops
began to collect from all quarters. At last we mustered about thirteen hundred strong, all mounted volunteers and all determined to
fight, judging from myself, for I felt wolfish all over. I verily believe
the whole army was of the real grit. Our captain didn't want any
other sort and to try them he several times told his men that if any
of them wanted to go back home they might do so at any time
before they were regularly mustered into the service. But he had
the honour to command all his men from first to last as not one of
them left him.

Gen'l. Jackson had not yet left Nashville with his old foot volunteers that had gone with him to Natchez in 1812, the year before.

While we remained at the spring, a Major Gibson came and wanted some volunteers to go with him across the Tennessee river and into the Creek nation, to find out the movements of the Indians. He came to my captain and asked for two of his best woodsmen and such as were best with a rifle. The captain pointed me out to him and said he would be security that I would go as far as the major would himself, or any other man. I willingly engaged to go with him and asked him to let me choose my own mate to go with me which he said I might do. I chose a young man by the name of George Russell, a son of old Major Russell, of Tennessee. I called him up, but Major Gibson said he thought he hadn't heard enough to please him, he wanted men and not boys. I must confess I was a little nettled at this, for I know'd George Russell and I know'd there was no mistake in him and I didn't think that courage ought to be measured by the beard for fear a goat would have the preference over a man. I told the major he was on the wrong scent; that Russell could go as far as he could and that I must have him along. He saw I was a little wrathy and said I had the best chance of knowing and agreed that it should be as I wanted it. He told us to be ready early in the morning for a start and so we were. We took our camp equipage, mounted our horses and, thirteen in number, including the major, we cut out. We went on and crossed the Tennessee river at a place called Ditto's Landing and then traveled about seven miles further and took up camp for the night. Here a man by the name of John Haynes overtook us. He had been an Indian trader in that part of the nation and was well acquainted with it. He went with us as a pilot. The next morning, however, Major Gibson and myself concluded we should separate and take different directions to see what discoveries we could make; so he took seven of the men and I five, making thirteen in all, including myself. He was to go by the house of a Cherokee Indian named Dick Brown and I was to go by Dick's father's and, getting all the information we could, we were to meet that evening where the roads came together, fifteen miles the other side of Brown's. At old Mr. Brown's I got a half blood Cherokee to agree to go with me, whose name was Jack Thompson. He was not then ready to start

but was to fix that evening and overtake us at the fork road where
I was to meet Major Gibson. I know'd it wouldn't be safe to camp
right at the road and so I told Jack that when he got to the fork he
must holler like an owl and I would answer him in the same way;
for I know'd it would be night before he got there. I and my men

then started and went on to the place of meeting. Major Gibson was not there. We waited till almost dark but still he didn't come. We then left the Indian trace a little distance and, turning into the head of a hollow, we struck up camp. It was about ten o'clock at night when I heard my owl and I answered him. Jack soon found us, and we determined to rest there during the night. We stayed also next morning till after breakfast but in vain, for the major didn't still come.

I told the men we had set out to hunt a fight and that we must go ahead and see what the red men were at. We started and went to a Cherokee town about twenty miles off and, after a short stay there, we pushed on to the house of a man by the name of Radcliff. He was a white man but had married a Creek woman and lived just in the edge of the Creek nation. He had two sons, large likely fellows, and a great deal of potatoes and corn and, indeed, almost every thing else to go on. We fed our horses and got dinner with him and seemed to be doing mighty well. But he was scared all the time. He told us there had been ten painted warriors at his house only an hour before and if we were discovered there, they would kill us and his family. I replied to him that my business was to hunt for just such fellows as he had described and I was determined not to go back until I had done it. Our dinner being over, we saddled up our horses and made ready to start. But some of my small company I found were disposed to return. I told them if we were to go back then, we should never hear the last of it and I was determined to go ahead. I knowed some of them would go with me and that the rest were afraid to go back by themselves and so we pushed on to the camp of some of the friendly Creeks, which was distant about eight miles. The moon was full and the night was clear. We therefore had the benefit of her light from night to morning and I knew if we were placed in such danger as to make a retreat necessary, we could travel by night as well as in the day time.

We had not gone very far when we met two negroes, well mounted on Indian ponies, and each with a good rifle. They had been taken from their owners by the Indians and were running away from them, trying to get back to their masters again. They were brothers, both very large and likely, and could talk Indian as well as English. One of them I sent on to Ditto's Landing, the other I took back with me. It was after dark when we got to the camp where we found about forty men, women, and children.

They had bows and arrows and I turned in to shooting with their boys by a pine light. In this way we amused ourselves very well for a while but at last the negro, who had been talking to the Indians, came to me and told me they were very much alarmed, for the "red sticks," as they called the war party of the Creeks, would come and find us there and, if so, we should all be killed. I directed him to tell them that I would watch, and if one would come that night, I would carry the skin of his head home to make me a mockasin. When he made this communication, the Indians laughed aloud. At about ten o'clock at night we all concluded to try to sleep a little but that our horses might be ready for use, as the treasurer said of the drafts on the United States' bank, on certain "Contingences," we tied them up with our saddles on them and every thing to our hand if in the night our quarters should get uncomfortable.

We lay down with our guns in our arms and I had just gotten into a dose of sleep when I heard the sharpest scream that ever escaped the throat of a human creature. It was more like a wrathy painter than any thing else. The negro understood it and he sprang to me; for tho' I heard the noise well enough, yet I wasn't wide awake enough to get up. So the negro caught me and said the red sticks was coming. I rose quicker then and asked what was the matter? Our negro had gone and talked with the Indian who had just fetched the scream as he come into camp and learned from him that the war party had been crossing the Coosa river all day at the Ten islands; and were going on to meet Jackson and this Indian had come as a runner. This news very much alarmed the friendly Indians in camp and they were all off in a few minutes. I felt bound to make this intelligence known as soon as possible to the army we had left at the landing and so we all mounted our horses and put out in a long loop to make our way back to that place. We were about sixty-five miles off. We went on to the same Cherokee town we had visited on our way out, having first called at Radclaff's, who was off with his family. At the the town we found large fires burning but not a single Indian was to be seen. They were all gone. These circumstances were calculated to lay our dander a little, as it appeared we must be in great danger; though we could easily have licked any force of not more than five to one. But we expected the whole nation would be on us and against such fearful odds we were not so rampant for a fight.

We therefore stayed only a short time in the light of the fires about the town, preferring the light of the moon and the shade of the woods. We pushed on till we got again to old Mr. Brown's, which was still about thirty miles from where we had left the main army. When we got there, the chickens were just at the first crowing for day. We fed our horses, got a morsel to eat ourselves, and again cut out. About ten o'clock in the morning we reached the camp and I reported to Colonel Coffee the news. He didn't seem to mind my report a bit and this raised my dander higher than ever but I knowed I had to be on my best behaviour, so I kept it all to myself, though I was so mad that I was burning inside like a tarkiln and I wonder that the smoke hadn't been pouring out of me at all points.

Major Gibson hadn't yet returned and we all began to think he was killed and that night they put out a double guard. The next day the major got in and brought a worse tale than I had, though he stated the same facts, so far as I went. This seemed to put our colonel all in a fidget and it convinced me, clearly, of one of the hateful ways of the world. When I made my report, it wasn't believed because I was no officer; I was no great man but just a poor soldier. But when the same thing was reported by Major Gibson why, then, it was all as true as preaching and the colonel believed it every word.

He, therefore, ordered breastworks to be thrown up near a quarter of a mile long and sent an express to Fayetteville, where General Jackson and his troops was, requesting them to push on like the very mischief for fear we should all be cooked up to a cracklin before they could get there. Old Hickory-face made a forced march on getting the news and, on the next day, he and his men got into camp with their feet all blistered from the effects of their swift journey. The volunteers, therefore, stood guard altogether to let them rest.

* * *

About eight hundred of the volunteers, and of that number I was one, were now sent back crossing the Tennessee river and on through Huntsville so as to cross the river again at another place to get the Indians in another direction. After we passed Huntsville, we struck on the river at the Muscle Shoals and at a place called Melton's Bluff. This river here is about two miles wide and a rough bottom; so much so, as to be dangerous. We left several of the horses belonging to our men, with their feet fast in the crevices of the rocks. The men, whose horses were thus left, went ahead on foot. We pushed on till we got to what was called the Black Warrior's town, which stood near the very spot where Tuscaloosa now stands, which is the seat of government for the state of Alabama.

This Indian town was a large one but when we arrived we found the Indians had all left it. There was a large field of corn standing out and a pretty good supply in some cribs. There was also a fine quantity of dried beans, which were very acceptable to us; and without delay we secured them as well as the corn and then burned the town to ashes, after which we left the place.

In the field where we gathered the corn we saw plenty of fresh Indian tracks and we had no doubt they had been scared off by our arrival.

We then went on to meet the main army at the fork road where I was first to have met Major Gibson. We got that evening as far back as the encampment we had made the night before we reached the Black Warrior's town, which had been destroyed. The next day we were entirely out of meat. I went to Col. Coffee, who was then in command of us, and asked his leave to hunt as we marched. He gave me leave, but told me to take mighty good care of myself. I turned aside to hunt, and had not gone far when I found a deer that had just been killed and skinned, and his flesh was still warm and smoking. From this I was sure that the Indian who had killed it had been gone only a very few minutes and though I was never much in favour of one hunter stealing from another, yet meat was so scarce in camp, that I thought I must go in for it. So I just took up the deer on my horse before me, and carried it on till night. I could have sold it for almost any price I would have asked; but this wasn't my rule, neither In peace nor war. Whenever I had any thing and saw a fellow suffering, I was more anxious to relieve him than to benefit myself. And this is one of the true secrets of my being a poor man to this day. But it is my way; and while it has often left me with an empty purse, which is as near the devil as any thing else I have seen, yet it has never left my heart empty of con-solations which money couldn't buy,—the consolations of having sometimes fed the hungry and covered the naked.

I gave all my deer away except a small part I kept for myself and just sufficient to make a good supper for my mess; for meat was getting to be a rarity to us all. We had to live mostly on parched corn. The next day we marched on and at night took up camp near a large cane brake. While here, I told my mess I would again try for some meat so I took my rifle and cut out, but hadn't gone far when I discovered a large gang of hogs. I shot one of them down in his tracks and the rest broke directly towards the camp. In a few min-utes, the guns began to roar as bad as if the whole army had been in an Indian battle; the hogs to squealing as bad as the pig did. I shouldered my hog, and went on to the camp and when I got there I found they had killed a good many of the hogs and a fine fat cow that had broke out of the cane brake. We did very well that night and the next morning marched on to a Cherokee town, where our officers stop'd and gave the inhabitants an order on Uncle Sam for their cow and the hogs we had killed. The next day we met the main army having had, as we thought, hard times and a plenty of them, though we had yet seen hardly the beginning of trouble.

After our meeting we went on to Radcliff's, where I had been before while out as a spy; and when we got there, we found he had hid all his provisions. We also got into the secret, that he was the very rascal who had sent the runner to the Indian camp with the news that the "red sticks" were crossing at the Ten Islands and that his object was to scare me and my men away, and send us back with a false alarm.

To make some atonement for this, we took the old scroundrell's two big sons with us and made them serve in the war.

We then marched to a place which we called Camp Wills and here it was that Captain Cannon was promoted to a colonel and Colonel Coffee to a general. We then marched to the Ten Islands on the Coosa river where we established a fort and our spy companies were sent out. They soon made prisoners of Bob Catala and his warriors and, in a few days afterwards, we heard of some Indians in a town about eight miles off. So we mounted our horses and put out for that town under the direction of two friendly Creeks we had taken for pilots. We had also a Cherokee colonel, Dick Brown, and some of his men with us. When we got near the town we divided; one of our pilots going with each division. And so we passed on each side of the town, keeping near to it, until our lines met on the far side. We then closed up at both ends so as to surround it completely and then we sent Captain Hammond's company of rangers to bring on the affray. He had advanced near the town, when the Indians saw him, and they raised the yell and came running at him like so many red devils. The main army was now formed in a hollow square around the town and they pursued Hammond till they came in reach of us. We then gave them a fire,

and they returned it, and then ran back into their town. We began to close on the town by making our files closer and closer, and the Indians soon saw they were our property. So most of them wanted us to take them prisoners and their squaws and all would run and take hold of any of us they could and give themselves up. I saw seven squaws have hold of one man, which made me think of the

Scriptures. So I hollered out the Scriptures was fulfilling, that there was seven women holding to one man's coat tail. But I believe it was a hunting-shirt all the time. We took them all prisoners that came out to us in this way but I saw some warriors run into a house until I counted forty-six of them. We pursued them until we got near the house when we saw a squaw sitting in the door. She placed her feet against the bow she had in her hand and then took an arrow and, raising her feet, she drew with all her might and let fly at us and she killed a man whose name, I believe, was Moore. He was a lieutenant and his death so enraged us all that she was fired on and had at least twenty balls blown through her. This was the first man I ever saw killed with a bow and arrow. We now shot them like dogs and then set the house on fire and burned it up with the forty-six warriors in it. I recollect seeing a boy who was shot down near the house. His arm and thigh was broken and he was so near the burning house that the grease was stewing out of him. In this situation he was still trying to crawl along but not a murmur escaped him, though he was only about twelve years old. So sullen is the Indian when his dander is up that he had sooner die than make a noise or ask for quarters.

The number that we took prisoners, being added to the number we killed, amounted to one hundred and eighty-six; though I don't remember the exact number of either. We had five of our men killed. We then returned to our camp, at which our fort was erected and known by the name of Fort Strother. No provisions had yet reached us and we had now been for several days on half rations. However we went back to our Indian town on the next day when many of the carcasses of the Indians were still to be seen. They looked very awful, for the burning had not entirely consumed them, but given them a very terrible appearance, at least what remained of them. It was, somehow or other, found out that the house had a potatoe cellar under it and an immediate examination was made, for we were all as hungry as wolves. We found a fine chance of potatoes in it, and hunger compelled us to eat them, though I had a little rather not, if I could have helped it, for the oil of the Indians we had burned up on the day before had run down on them and they looked like they had been stewed with fat meat. We then again returned to the army and remained there for several days almost starving, as all our beef was gone. We commenced eating the beef-hides and continued to eat every scrap we could lay our hands on. At length an Indian came to our guard one night and hollered and said he wanted to see "Captain Jackson." He was conducted to the general's markee, into which he entered, and in a few minutes we received orders to prepare for marching.

In an hour we were all ready and took up the line of march. We crossed the Coosa river and went on in the direction to Fort Taladega. When we arrived near the place, we met eleven hundred painted warriors, the very choice of the Creek nation. They had encamped near the fort and had informed the friendly Indians who were in it that if they didn't come out and fight with them against the whites, they would take their fort and all their ammunition and provision. The friendly party asked three days to consider of it and agreed that if on the third day they didn't come out ready to fight with them, they might take their fort. Thus they put them off. They then immediately started their runner to General Jackson and he and the army pushed over, as I have just before stated.

The camp of warriors had their spies out and discovered us coming some time before we got to the fort. They then went to the friendly Indians and told them Captain Jackson was coming and had a great many fine horses and blankets and guns and every thing else; and if they would come out and help to whip him, and to take his plunder, it should all be divided with those in the fort. They promised that when Jackson came, they would then come out and help to whip him. It was about an hour by sun in the morning when we got near the fort. We were piloted by friendly Indians and divided as we had done on a former occasion, so as to go to the right and left of the fort and, consequently, of the warriors who were camped near it. Our lines marched on as before till they met in front and then closed in the rear, forming again into a hollow square. We then sent on old Major Russell, with his spy company, to bring on the battle; Capt. Evans' company went also. When they got near the fort, the top of it was lined with the friendly Indians crying out as loud as they could roar, "How-dy-do, brother, how-dy-do?" They kept this up till Major Russel had passed by the fort and was moving on towards the warriors. They were all painted as red as scarlet and were just as naked as they were born. They had concealed themselves under the bank of a branch that ran partly around the fort in the manner of a half moon. Russel was going right into their circle, for he couldn't see them, while the Indians on the top of the fort were trying every plan to show him his danger. But he couldn't understand them. At last, two of them jumped from it and ran and took his horse by the bridle and, pointing to where they were, told him there were thousands of them lying under the bank. This brought them to a halt and about this moment the Indians fired on them and came rushing forth like a cloud of Egyptian locusts, screaming like all the young devils had been turned loose, with the old devil of all at their head. Russel's company quit their horses and took into the fort and their horses ran up to our line, which was then in full view. The warriors then came yelling on, meeting us, and continued till they were within shot of us, when we fired and killed a considerable number of them. They then broke like a gang of steers and ran across to our other line where they were again fired on. We kept them running from one line to the other, constantly under a heavy fire, until we had killed upwards of four hundred of them. They fought with guns and also with their bows and arrows, but at length they made their escape through a part of our line which was made up of drafted militia, which broke ranks, and they passed. We lost fifteen of our men, as brave fellows as ever lived or died. We buried them all in one grave and started back to our fort but before we got there, two more of our men died of wounds they had received, making our total loss seventeen good fellows in that battle.

We now remained at the fort a few days but no provision came yet and we were all likely to perish. The weather also began to get very cold and our clothes were nearly worn out and horses getting very feeble and poor. Our officers proposed to Gen'l. Jackson to let us return home and get fresh horses and fresh clothing so as to be better prepared for another campaign, for our sixty days had long been out and that was the time we entered for.

But the general took "the responsibility" on himself and refused. We were, however, determined to go, as I am to put back the deposites, if I can. With this, the general issued his orders against it, as he has against the bank. But we began to fix for a start, as provisions were too scarce; just as Clay and Webster and myself are preparing to fix bank matters on account of the scarcity of money. The general went and placed his cannon on a bridge we had to cross and ordered out his regulars and drafted men to keep us from crossing; just as he has planted his Globe and K. C. to alarm the bank men, while his regulars and militia in Congress are to act as artillery men. But when the militia started to guard the bridge, they would holler back to us to bring their knapsacks along when we come, for they wanted to go as bad as we did; just as many a good fellow now wants his political knapsack brought along, that if, when we come to vote, he sees he has a fair shake to go, he may join in and help us to take back the deposites.

We got ready and moved on till we came near the bridge where the general's men were all strung along on both sides, just like the officeholders are now, to keep us from getting along to the help of the country and the people. But we all had our flints ready picked and our guns ready primed, that if we were fired on we might fight our way through or all die together, just as we are now determined to save the country from ready ruin or to sink down with it. When we came still nearer the bridge we heard the guards cocking their guns and we did the same; just as we have had it in Congress, while the "government" regulars and the people's volunteers have all been setting their political triggers. But, after all, we marched boldly on and not a gun was fired, nor a life lost; just as I hope it will be again that we shall not be afraid of the general's Globe, nor his K. C. nor his regulars, nor their trigger snapping; but just march boldly over the executive bridge and take the deposites back where the law placed them and where they ought to be. When we had passed, no further attempt was made to stop us but the general said, we were "the damned'st volunteers he had ever seen in his life; that we would volunteer and go out and fight and then, at our pleasure would volunteer and go home again, in spite of the devil." But we went on; and near Huntsvile we met a reinforcement who were going on to join the army. It consisted of a regiment of volunteers and was under the command of someone whose name I can't remember. They were sixty-day volunteers.

We got home pretty safely and in a short time we had procured fresh horses and a supply of clothing better suited for the season and then we returned to Fort Deposite, where our officers held a sort of a "national convention" on the subject of a message they had received from General Jackson, demanding that on our return we should serve out six months. We had already served three months instead of two, which was the time we had volunteered for. The next morning the officers reported to us the conclusions they had come to and told us if any of us felt bound to go on and serve out the six months we could do so but that they intended to go back home. I knowed if I went back home I couldn't rest, for I felt it my duty to be out and when out was, somehow or other, always delighted to be in the very thickest of the danger. A few of us, therefore, determined to push on and join the army. The number I do not recollect, but it was very small.

When we got out there, I joined Major Russel's company of spies. Before we reached the place, General Jackson had started. We went on likewise and overtook him at a place where we established a fort called Fort Williams and leaving men to guard it, we went ahead intending to go to a place called the Horse-shoe bend of the Talapoosa river. When we came near that place, we began to find Indian sign plenty and we struck up camp for the night. About two hours before day, we heard our guard firing, and we were all up in little or no time. We mended up our camp fires and then fell back in the dark, expecting to see the Indians pouring in and intending, when they should do so, to shoot them by the light of our own fires. But it happened that they did not rush in as we

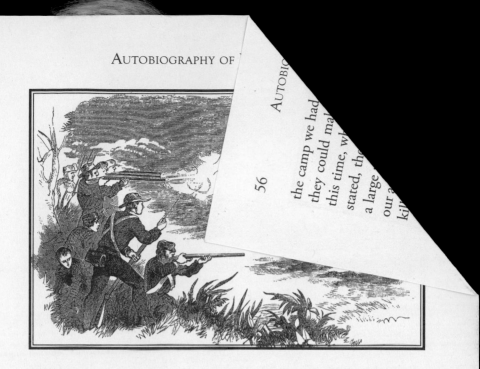

56

Autobio

the camp we had

they could ma

this time, wh

stated, the

a large

our

kil

had expected, but commenced a fire on us as we were. We were encamped in a hollow square and we not only returned the fire, but continued to shoot as well as we could in the dark till day broke, when the Indians disappeared, The only guide we had in shooting was to notice the flash of their guns and then shoot as directly at the place as we could guess.

In this scrape we had four men killed and several wounded; but whether we killed any of the Indians or not we never could tell, for it is their custom always to carry off their dead if they can possibly do so. We buried ours and then made a large log heap over them and set it on fire so that the place of their deposite might not be known to the savages, who, we knew, would seek for them, that they might scalp them. We made some horse litters for our wounded and took up a retreat. We moved on till we came to a large creek which we had to cross. About half of our men had crossed when the Indians commenced firing on our left wing, and they kept it up very warmly. We had left Major Russel and his brother at moved from that morning to see what discovery ... e as to the movements of the Indians and, about ... ile a warm fire was kept up on our left, as I have just ... major came up in our rear and was closely pursued by ... umber of Indians who immediately commenced a fire on ... rtillery men. They hid themselves behind a large log and could ... one of our men almost every shot, they being in open ground and exposed. The worst of all was two of our colonels just at this trying moment left their men and, by a forced march, crossed the creek out of the reach of the fire. Their names, at this late day, would do the world no good and my object is history alone and not the slightest interference with character. An opportunity was now afforded for Governor Carroll to distinguish himself and on this occasion he did so by greater bravery than I ever saw any other man display. In truth, I believe, as firmly as I do that General Jackson is president, that if it hadn't been for Carroll, we should all have been genteely licked that time, for we were in a devil of a fix; part of our men on one side of the creek and part on the other and the Indians all the time pouring it on us, as hot as fresh mustard to a sore shin. I will not say exactly that the old general was whip'd but I will say that if we escaped it at all, it was like old Henry Snider going to heaven, "mita tam tite squeeze." I think he would confess himself that he was nearer whip'd this time than he was at any other, for I know that all the world couldn't make him acknowledge that he was pointedly whip'd. I know I was mighty glad when it was over and the savages quit us, for I had begun to think there was one behind every tree in the woods.

We buried our dead, the number of whom I have also forgotten, and again made horse litters to carry our wounded and so we put out and returned to Fort Williams, from which place we had started. In the mean time, my horse had got crippled and was unfit for service and as another reinforcement had arrived, I thought they could get along without me for a short time so I got a furlough and went home, for we had had hard times again on this hunt and I began to feel as though I had done Indian fighting enough for one time. I remained at home until after the army had returned to the Horse-shoe bend and fought the battle there. But not being with them at that time, of course no history of that fight can be expected of me.

* * *

Soon after this, an army was to be raised to go to Pensacola and I determined to go again with them, for I wanted a small taste of British fighting and I supposed they would be there.

Here again the entreaties of my wife were thrown in the way of my going, but all in vain; for I always had a way of just going ahead at whatever I had a mind to. One of my neighbhours, hearing I had determined to go, came to me and offered me a hundred dollars to go in his place as a substitute, as he had been drafted. I told him I was better raised than to hire myself out to be shot at but that I would go and he should go too and in that way the government would have the services of us both. But we didn't call General Jackson "the government" in those days, though we used to go and fight under him in the war.

I fixed up and joined old Major Russel again but we couldn't start with the main army but followed on, in a little time, after them. In a day or two, we had a hundred and thirty men in our company and we went over and crossed the Muscle Shoals at the same place where I had crossed when first out and when we burned the Black Warriors' town. We passed through the Choctaw and Chickesaw nations, on to Fort Stephens, and from thence to what is called the Cut-off, at the junction of the Tom-Bigby with the Alabama river. This place is near the old Fort Mimms, where the Indians committed the great butchery at the commencement of the war.

We were here about two days behind the main army who had left their horses at the Cut-off and taken it on foot. They did this because there was no chance for forage between there and Pensacola. We did the same, leaving men enough to take care of our horses, and cut out on foot for that place. It was about eighty miles off but in good heart we shouldered our guns, blankets, and provisions and trudged merrily on. About twelve o'clock the second day, we reached the encampment of the main army, which was situated on a hill overlooking the city of Pensacola. My commander, Major Russel, was a great favourite with Gen'l. Jackson and our arrival was hailed with great applause, though we were a little after the feast for they had taken the town and fort before we got there. That evening we went down into the town and could see the British fleet lying in sight of the place. We got some liquor and took a "horn" or so and went back to the camp. We remained there that night and in the morning we marched back towards the Cut-off. We pursued this direction till we reached old Fort Mimms where we remained two or three days. It was here that Major Russel was promoted from his command, which was only that of a captain of spies, to the command of a major in the line. He had been known long before at home as old Major Russel, and so we all continued to call him in the army. A Major Childs, from East Tennessee, also commanded a battalion, and his and the one Russel was now appointed to command composed a regiment, which, by agreement with General Jackson, was to quit his army and go to the south to kill up the Indians on the Scamby river.

General Jackson and the main army set out the next morning for New Orleans and a Colonel Blue took command of the regiment which I have before described. We remained, however, a few days after the general's departure and then started also on our route.

As it gave rise to so much war and bloodshed, it may not be improper here to give a little description of Fort Mimms and the manner in which the Indian war commenced. The fort was built right in the middle of a large old field and in it the people had been forted so long and so quietly, that they didn't apprehend any danger at all and had, therefore, become quite careless. A small negro boy, whose business it was to bring up the calves at milking time, had been out for that purpose and on coming back, he said he saw a great many Indians. At this the inhabitants took the alarm and closed their gates and placed out their guards, which they continued for a few days. But finding that no attack was made, they concluded the little negro had lied and again threw their gates open and set all their hands out to work their fields. The same boy was out again on the same errand, when, returning in great haste and alarm, he informed them that he had seen the Indians as thick as trees in the woods. He was not believed, but was tucked up to receive a flogging for the supposed lie and was actually getting badly licked at the very moment when the Indians came in a troop, loaded with rails, with which they stop'd all the port-holes of the fort on one side except the bastion, and then they fell in to cutting down the picketing. Those inside the fort had only the bastion to shoot from, as all the other holes were spiked up, and they shot several of the Indians while engaged in cutting. But as fast as one would fall, another would seize up the axe and chop away until they succeeded in cutting down enough of the picketing to admit them to enter. They then began to rush through and continued until they were all in. They immediately commenced scalping, without regard to age or sex; having forced the inhabitants up to one side of the fort, where they carried on the work of death as a butcher would in a slaughter pen.

The scene was particularly described to me by a young man who was in the fort when it happened and subsequently went on with

us to Pensacola. He said that he saw his father and mother, his four sisters and the same number of brothers, all butchered in the most shocking manner and that he made his escape by running over the heads of the crowd, who were against the fort wall, to the top of the fort, and then jumping off, taking to the woods. He was closely pursued by several Indians until he came to a small bayou, across which there was a log. He knew the log was hollow on the under side so he slip'd under the log and hid himself. He said he heard the Indians walk over him several times back and forward. He remained, nevertheless, still till night when he came out and finished his escape. The name of this young man has entirely escaped my recollection, though his tale greatly excited my feelings. But to return to my sub-ject. The regiment marched from where Gen'l. Jackson had left us to Fort Montgomery, which was distant from Fort Mimms about a mile and a half, where we remained for some days.

Here we supplied ourselves pretty well with beef, by killing wild cattle which had formerly belonged to the people who perished in the fort, but had gone wild after their massacre.

When we marched from Fort Montgomery, we went some dis-tance back towards Pensacola, then we turned to the left and passed through a poor piny country till we reached the Scamby river, near which we encamped. We had about one thousand men and as a part of that number, one hundred and eighty-six Chickesaw and Choctaw Indians with us. That evening a boat landed from Pensacola, bringing many articles that were both good and necessary, such as sugar and coffee and liquors of all kinds. The same evening, the Indians we had along proposed to cross the river, and the officers thinking it might be well for them to do so, consented and Major Russell went with them, taking sixteen white men, of which number I was one. We camped on the opposite bank that night and early in the morning we set out. We had not gone far before we came to a place where the whole country was covered with water and looked like a sea. We didn't stop for this, tho', but just put in like so many spaniels, and waded on, sometimes up to our armpits, until we reached the pine hills, which made our distance through the water about a mile and a half. Here we struck up a fire to warm ourselves, for it was cold, and we were chilled through by being so long in the water. We again moved on, keeping our spies out; two to our left near the bank of the river, two straight before us, and two others on our right. We had gone in this way about six miles up the river when our spies on the left came to us leaping the brush like so many old bucks, and informed us that they had discovered a camp of Creek Indians and that we must kill them. Here we paused for a few minutes and the prophets pow-wowed over their men awhile, and then got out their paint and painted them, all according to their custom when going into battle. They then brought their paint to old Major Russell and said to him that as he was an officer and must be painted too. He agreed and they painted him just as they had done themselves. We let the Indians understand that we white men would first fire on the camp, and then fall back, so as to give the Indians a chance to rush in and scalp them. The Chickasaws marched on our left hand, the Choctaws on our right, and we moved on till we got in hearing of the camp, where the Indians were employed in beating up what they called chainy briar root. On this they mostly subsisted. On a nearer approach we found they were on an island and that we could not get to them.

While we were chatting about this matter, we heard some guns fired and, in a very short time after a keen whoop, which satisfied us that whereever it was, there was war on a small scale. With that we all broke, like quarter horses, for the firing and when we got there we found it was our two front spies who related to us the following story: As they were moving on, they had met with two Creeks who were out hunting their horses; as they approached each other, there was a large cluster of green bay bushes exactly between them so that they were within a few feet of meeting before either was discovered. Our spies walked up to them and, speaking in the Shawnee tongue, informed them that General Jackson was at Pensacola and they were making their escape and wanted to know where they could get something to eat. The Creeks told them that nine miles up the Conaker, the river they were then on, there was a large camp of Creeks and they had cattle and plenty to eat and further, that their own camp was on an island about a mile off just below the mouth of the Conaker. They held their conversation and struck up a fire and smoked together, shook hands and parted. One of the Creeks had a gun, the other had none, and as soon as they had parted, our Choctaws turned round and shot down the one that had the gun, and the other attempted to run off. They snapped several times at him, but the gun still missing fire, they took after him, and overtaking him, one of them struck him over the head with his gun and followed up his blows till he killed him.

The gun was broken in the combat and they then fired off the gun of the Creek they had killed and raised the war-whoop. When we reached them, they had cut off the heads of both the Indians and each of those Indians with us would walk up to one of the heads and, taking his war club, would strike on it. This was done by every one of them and when they had got done, I took one of their clubs and walked up as they had done and struck it on the head also. At this they all gathered round me and, patting me on the shoulder, would call me "Warrior—warrior."

They scalped the heads and then we moved on a short distance to where we found a trace leading in towards the river. We took this trace and pursued it till we came to where a Spaniard had been killed and scalped together with a woman, who we supposed to be his wife, and also four children. I began to feel mighty ticklish along about this time, for I knowed if there was no danger then, there had been; and I felt exactly like there still was. We, however, went on till we struck the river and then continued down it till we came opposite to the Indian camp, where we found they were still beating their roots.

It was now late in the evening and they were in a thick cane brake. We had some few friendly Creeks with us, who said they could decoy them. So we all hid behind trees and logs, while the attempt was made. The Indians would not agree that we should fire, but pick'd out some of their best gunners, and placed them near the river. Our Creeks went down to the river's side and hailed the camp in the Creek language. We heard an answer, and an Indian man started down towards the river but didn't come in sight. He went back and again commenced beating his roots and sent a squaw. She came down and talked with our Creeks until dark came on. They told her they wanted her to bring them a canoe. To which she replied that their canoe was on our side. that two of their men had gone out to hunt their horses and hadn't yet returned. They were the same two we had killed. The canoe was found and forty of our picked Indian warriors were crossed over to take the camp. There was at last only one man in it. He escaped and they took two squaws and ten children, but killed none of them, of course.

We had run nearly out of provisions and Major Russell had determined to go up the Conaker to the camp we had heard of from the Indians we had killed. I was one that he selected to go down the river that night for provisions with the canoe to where we had left our regiment. I took with me a man by the name of John Guess and one of the friendly Creeks and cut out. It was very dark and the river was so full that it overflowed the banks and the adjacent low bottoms. This rendered it very difficult to keep the channel and particularly as the river was very crooked. At about ten o'clock at night we reached the camp and were to return by morning to Major Russell with provisions for his trip up the river, but on informing Colonel Blue of this arrangement, he vetoed it as quick as General Jackson did the bank bill and said, if Major Russell didn't come back the next day, it would be bad times for him. I found we were not to go up the Conaker to the Indian camp and a man of my company offered to go up in my place to inform Major Russell. I let him go and they reached the major, as I was told, about sunrise in the morning, who immediately returned with those who were with him to the regiment and joined us where we crossed the river, as hereafter stated.

The next morning we all fixed up and marched down the Scamby to a place called Miller's Landing where we swam our horses across and sent on two companies down on the side of the bay opposite to Pensacola, where the Indians had fled when the main army first marched to that place. One was the company of Captain William Russell, a son of the old major, and the other was commanded by a Captain Trimble. They went on and had a little skirmish with the Indians. They killed some and took all the balance prisoners, though I don't remember the numbers. We again met those companies in a day or two and sent the prisoners they had taken on to Fort Montgomery, in charge of some of our Indians.

I did hear that after they left us, the Indians killed and scalped all the prisoners and I never heard the report contradicted. I cannot positively say it was true, but I think it entirely probable, for it is very much like the Indian character.

* * *

WHEN we made a move from the point where we met the companies, we set out for Chatahachy, the place for which we had
started when we left Fort Montgomery. At the start we had taken
only twenty days' rations of flour, and eight days' rations of beef;
and it was now thirty-four days before we reached that place. We
were, therefore, in extreme suffering for want of something to eat,
and exhausted with our exposure and the fatigues of our journey.
I remember well, that I had not myself tasted bread but twice in
nineteen days. I had bought a pretty good supply of coffee from the
boat that had reached us from Pensacola, on the Scamby, and on
that we chiefly subsisted. At length, one night our spies came in,
and informed us they had found Holm's village on the Chatahachy
river; and we made an immediate push for that place. We traveled

all night, expecting to get something to eat when we got there. We arrived about sunrise and near the place prepared for battle. We were all so furious that even the certainty of a pretty hard fight could not have restrained us. We made a furious charge on the town but to our great mortification and surprise, there wasn't a human being in it. The Indians had all run off and left it. We burned the town, however; but, melancholy to tell, we found no provision whatever. We then turned about, and went back to the camp we had left the night before as nearly starved as any set of poor fellows ever were in the world.

We staid there only a little while when we divided our regiment, and Major Childs, with his men, went back the way we had come for a considerable distance and then turned to Baton-Rouge, where they joined General Jackson and the main army on their return from Orleans. Major Russell and his men struck for Fort Decatur, on the Talapoosa river. Some of our friendly Indians, who knew the country, went on ahead of us, as we had no trail except the one they made to follow. With them we sent some of our ablest horses and men to get us some provisions to prevent us from absolutely starving to death. As the army marched, I hunted every day and would kill every hawk, bird, and squirrel that I could find. Others did the same; and it was a rule with us, that when we stop'd at night, the hunters would throw all they killed in a pile and then we would make a general division among all the men. One evening I came in, having killed nothing that day. I had a very sick man in my mess and I wanted something for him to eat, even if I starved myself. So I went to the fire of a Captain Cowen, who commanded my company after the promotion of Major Russell, and informed him that I was on the hunt of something for a sick man to eat. I knowed the captain was as bad off as the rest of us but I found him broiling a turkey's gizzard. He said he had divided the turkey out among the sick, that Major Smiley had killed it, and that nothing else had been killed that day. I immediately went to Smiley's fire, where I found him broiling another gizzard. I told him that it was the first turkey I had ever seen have two gizzards. But so it was, I got nothing for my sick man. And now seeing that every fellow must shift for himself, I determined that in the morning, I would come up missing, so I took my mess and cut out to go ahead of the army. We know'd that nothing more could happen to us if we went than if we stayed, for it looked like it was to be starvation any way; we therefore determined to go on the old saying, root hog or die. We passed two camps, at which our men that had gone on before us, had killed Indians. At one they had killed nine, and at the other three. About daylight we came to a small river, which I thought was the Scamby but we continued on for three days, killing little or nothing to eat till, at last, we all began to get nearly ready to give up the ghost and lie down and die, for we had no prospect of provision and we knew we couldn't go much further without it.

We came to a large prairie that was about six miles across it and in this I saw a trail which I knowed was made by bear, deer, and turkeys. We went on through it till we came to a large creek and the low grounds were all set over with wild rye, looking as green as a wheat field. We here made a halt, unsaddled our horses and turned them loose to graze.

One of my companions, a Mr. Vanzant, and myself, then went up the low grounds to hunt. We had gone some distance, finding nothing when at last I found a squirrel which I shot, but he got into a hole in the tree. The game was small, but necessity is not very particular so I thought I must have him and I climbed that tree thirty feet high, without a limb, and pulled him out of his hole. I shouldn't relate such small matters, only to show what lengths a hungry man will go to to get something to eat. I soon killed two other squirrels and fired at a large hawk. At this a large gang of turkeys rose from the cane brake and flew across the creek to where my friend was, who had just before crossed it. He soon fired on a large gobler and I heard it fall. By this time my gun was loaded again, and I saw one sitting on my side of the creek which had flew over when he fired so I blazed away and down I brought him. I gathered him up, a fine turkey he was. I now began to think we had struck a breeze of luck and almost forgot our past sufferings in the prospect of once more having something to eat. I raised the shout and my comrade came to me and we went on to our camp with the game we had killed. While we were gone, two of our mess had been out and each of them had found a bee tree. We turned into cooking some of our game but we had neither salt nor bread. Just at this moment, on looking down the creek, we saw our men who had gone on before us for provisions coming to us. They came up and measured out to each man a cupfull of flower. With this, we thickened our soup when our turkey was cooked and our friends took dinner with us and then went on.

We now took our tomahawks and went and cut our bee-trees, out of which we got a fine chance of honey; though we had been starving so long that we feared to eat much at a time, till, like the Irish by hanging, we got used to it again. We rested that night without moving our camp and the next morning myself and Vanzant again turned out to hunt. We had not gone far before I wounded a fine buck very badly and, while pursuing him, I was walking on a large tree that had fallen down when, from the top of it, a large bear broke out and ran off. I had no dogs and I was sorry enough for it, for of all the hunting I ever did, I have always delighted most in bear hunting. Soon after this, I killed a large buck and we had just gotten him to camp when our poor starved army came up. They told us that to lessen their sufferings as much as possible, Captain William Russell had had his horse led up to be shot for them to eat just at the moment that they saw our men returning, who had carried on the flour.

We were now about fourteen miles from Fort Decatur and we gave away all our meat and honey and went on with the rest of the army. When we got there, they could give us only one ration of meat but not a mouthful of bread. I immediately got a canoe, and taking my gun, crossed over the river and went to the Big Warrior's town. I had a large hat and I offered an Indian a silver dollar for my hat full of corn. He told me that his corn was all "*shuestea*," which in English means it was all gone. But he showed me where an Indian lived, who, he said, had corn. I went to him and made the same offer. He could talk a little broken English and he said to me, "You got any powder? You got bullet?" I told him I had. He then said, "Me swap my corn for powder and bullet." I took out about ten bullets and showed him and he proposed to give me a hat full of corn for them. I took him up mighty quick. I then offered to give him ten charges of powder for another hat full of corn. To this he agreed very willingly. So I took off my hunting-shirt and tied up my corn and though it had cost me very little of my powder and lead, I wouldn't have taken fifty silver dollars for it. I returned to the camp and the next morning we started for the Hickory Ground, which was thirty miles off. It was here that General Jackson met the Indians and made peace with the body of the nation.

We got nothing to eat at this place and we had yet to go forty-nine miles over a rough and wilderness country to Fort Williams. Parched corn, and but little even of that, was our daily subsistence. When we reached Fort Williams, we got one ration of pork and one of flour, which was our only hope until we could reach Fort Strother.

The horses were now giving out and I remember to have seen thirteen good horses left in one day, the saddles and bridles being thrown away. It was thirty-nine miles to Fort Strother and we had to pass directly by Fort Talladego, where we first had the big Indian battle with the eleven hundred painted warriors. We went through the old battle ground and it looked like a great gourd patch, the skulls of the Indians who were killed still lay scattered all about, many of their frames were still perfect as the bones had not separated. But about five miles before we got to this battle ground, I struck a trail which I followed until it led me to one of their towns. Here I swap'd some more of my powder and bullets for a little corn.

I pursued on, by myself, till some time after night, when I came up with the rest of the army. That night my company and myself did pretty well as I divided out my corn among them. The next morning we met the East Tennessee troops, who were on their road to Mobile, and my youngest brother was with them. They had plenty of corn and provisions and they gave me what I wanted for myself and my horse. I remained with them that night, though my company went across the Coosa river to the fort, where they also had the good fortune to find plenty of provisions. Next morning, I took leave of my brother and all my old neighbours, for there were a good many of them with him, and crossed over to my men at the fort. Here I had enough to go on, and after remaining a few days, cut out for home. Nothing more, worthy of the reader's attention, transpired till I was safely landed at home once more with my wife and children. I found them all well and doing well, though I was only a rough sort of a backwoodsman, they seemed mighty glad to see me, however little the quality folks might suppose it. For I do reckon we love as hard in the backwood country as any people in the whole reation.

But I had been home only a few days when we received orders to start again and go on to the Black Warrior and Cahawba rivers to see if there was no Indians there. I know'd well enough there was none and I wasn't willing to trust my craw any more where there was neither any fighting to do, nor any thing to go on; and so I agreed to give a young man, who wanted to go, the balance of my wages if he would serve out my time, which was about a month. He did so and when they returned, sure enough they hadn't seen an Indian any more than if they had been all the time chopping wood in my clearing. This closed my career as a warrior and I am glad of it, for I like life now a heap better than I did then and I am glad all over that I lived to see these times, which I should not have done if I had kept fooling along in war and got used up at it. When I say I am glad, I just mean I am glad I am alive, for there is a confounded heap of things I ain't glad of at all. I ain't glad, for example, that the "government" moved the deposites, and if my military glory should take such a turn as to make me president after the general's time, I' ll move them back; yes, I, the "government," will "take the responsibility," and move them back again. If I don't, I wish I may be shot.

But I am glad that I am now through war matters, and I reckon the reader is too, for they have no fun in them at all and less if he had had to pass through them first, and then to write them afterwards. But for the dullness of their narrative, I must try to make amends by relating some of the curious things that happened to me in private life, and when forced to become a public man, as I shall have to be again, if ever I consent to take the presidential chair.

* * *

I CONTINUED at home now, working my farm for two years, as the war finally closed soon after I quit the service. The battle at New Orleans had already been fought and treaties were made with the Indians which put a stop to their hostilities.

But in this time, I met with the hardest trial which ever falls to the lot of man. Death, that cruel leveller of all distinctions, to whom the prayers and tears of husbands, and of even helpless infancy, are addressed invain, entered my humble cottage and tore from my children an affectionate good mother and from me a tender and loving wife.

It is a scene long gone by and one which it would be supposed I had almost forgotten, yet when I turn my memory back on it, it seems as but the work of yesterday. It was the doing of the Almighty, whose ways are always right, though we sometimes think they fall heavily on us and as painful as is even yet the remembrance of her sufferings, and the loss sustained by my little children and myself, yet I have no wish to lift up the voice of complaint. I was left with three children; the two oldest were sons, the youngest a daughter and, at that time, a mere infant. It appeared to me, at that moment, that my situation was the worst in the world. I couldn't bear the thought of scattering my children and so I got my youngest brother, who was also married, and his family, to live with me. They took as good care of my children as they well could but yet it wasn't all like the care of a mother. And though their company was to me in every respect like that of a brother and sister, yet it fell far short of being like that of a wife. So I came to the conclusion it wouldn't do but that I must have another wife.

There lived in the neighbourhood a widow lady whose husband had been killed in the war. She had two children, a son and daughter, and both quite small, like my own. I began to think that as we were both in the same situation, it might be that we could do something for each other and I therefore began to hint a little around the matter, as we were once and a while together. She was a good industrious woman, she owned a snug little farm and lived quite comfortable. I soon began to pay my respects to her in real good earnest but I was as sly as a fox when he is going to rob a hen-roost. I found that my company wasn't at all disagreeable to her and I thought I could treat her children with so much friendship as to make her a good stepmother to mine and in this I wan't mistaken, as we soon bargained and got married, and then went ahead. In a great deal of peace we raised our first crop of children, and they are all married and doing well. But we had a second crop together; and I shall notice them as I go along, as my wife and myself both had a hand in them, and they therefore belong to the history of my second marriage.

The next fall after this marriage, three of my neighbours and myself determined to explore a new country. Their names were Robinson, Frazier, and Rich. We set out for the Creek country, crossing the Tennessee river and after having made a day's travel, we stop'd at the house of one of my old acquaintances who had settled there after the war. Resting here a day, Frazier turned out to hunt, being a great hunter, but he got badly bit by a very poisonous snake so we left him and went on. We passed through a large rich valley, called Jones's valley, where several other families had settled, and continued our course till we came near to the place where Tuscaloosa now stands. Here we camped, as there were no inhabitants, and hobbled out our horses for the night. About two hours before day, we heard the bells on our horses going back the way we had come, as they had started to leave us. As soon as it was daylight, I started in pursuit of them on foot, and carrying my rifle, which was a very heavy one, I went ahead the whole day, wading creeks and swamps and climbing mountains but I couldn't overtake our horses, though I could hear of them at every house they passed. I at last found I couldn't catch up with them and so I gave up the hunt and turned back to the last house I had passed and stayed there till morning. From the best calculation we could make, I had walked over fifty miles that day and the next morning I was so sore and fatigued that I felt like I couldn't walk any more. But I was anxious to get back to where I had left my company and so I started and went on, but mighty slowly, till after the middle of the day. I now began to feel mighty sick and had a dreadful head-ache. My rifle was so heavy and I felt so weak that I lay down by the side of the trace, in a perfect wilderness too, to see if I wouldn't get better. In a short time some Indians came along. They had some ripe melons and wanted me to eat some, but I was so sick I couldn't. They then signed to me that I would die and be buried; a thing I was confoundedly afraid of myself. But I asked them how near it was to any house? By their signs, again, they made me understand it was a mile and a half. I got up to go but when I rose, I reeled about like a cow with the blind staggers, or a fellow who had taken too many "horns." One of the Indians proposed to go with me and carry my gun. I gave him half a dollar and accepted his offer. We got to the house, by which time I was pretty far gone but was kindly received and got on to a bed. The woman did all she could for me with her warm teas but I still continued bad enough with a high fever and generally out of my senses. The next day two of my neighbours were passing the road and heard of my situation. They came to where I was. They were going nearly the route I had intended to go to look at the country and so they took me first on one of their horses and then on the other till they got me back to where I had left my company. I expected I would get better and be able to go on with them, but, instead of this, I got worse and worse; and when we got there, I wan't able to sit up at all. I thought now the jig was mighty nigh up with me but I determined to keep a stiff upper lip. They carried me to a house and each of my comrades bought him a horse and they all set out together, leaving me behind. I knew but little that was going on for about two weeks but the family treated me with every possible kindness in their power and I shall always feel thankful to them. The man's name was Jesse Jones. At the end of two weeks I began to mend without the help of a doctor or of any doctor's means. In this time, however, as they told me, I was speechless for five days and they had no thought that I would ever speak again, in Congress or any where else. And so the woman, who had a bottle of Bates-man's draps, thought if they killed me, I would only die any how and so she would try it with me. She gave me the whole bottle, which throwed me into a sweat that continued on me all night, when at last I seemed to make up, and spoke, and asked her for a drink of water. This almost alarmed her, for she was looking every minute for me to die. She gave me the water and, from that time, I began slowly to mend and so kept on till I was able at last to walk about a little. I might easily have been mistaken for one of the Kitchen Cabinet, I looked so much like a ghost. I have been particular in giving a history of this sickness, not because I believe it will interest any body much now, nor, indeed, do I certainly know that it ever will. But if I should be forced to take the "white house" then it will be good history and every one will look on it as important. And I can't, for my life, help laughing now, to think that when all my folks get around me, wanting good fat offices, how so many of them will say, "What a good thing it was that that kind woman had the bottle of draps that saved President CROCKETT's life, the second greatest and best"!! Good, says I, my noble fellow! You take the post office or the navy or the war office or may-be the treasury. But if I give him the treasury, there's no devil if I don't make him agree first to fetch back them deposites. And if it's even the post-office, I'll make him promise to keep his money' counts without any figuring, as that throws the whole concern heels over head in debt in little or no time.

But when I got so I could travel a little, I got a waggoner who was passing along to hawl me to where he lived, which was about twenty miles from my house. I still mended as we went along and when we got to his stopping place, I hired one of his horses and went on home. I was so pale and so much reduced, that my face looked like it had been half soled with brown paper.

When I got there, it was to the utter astonishment of my wife, for she supposed I was dead. My neighbours who had started with me had returned and took my horse home, which they had found with their's, and they reported that they had seen men who had helped to bury me and who saw me draw my last breath. I know'd this was a whapper of a lie as soon as I heard it. My wife had hired a man and sent him out to see what had become of my money and other things; but I had missed the man as I went in and he didn't return until some time after I got home, as he went all the way to where I lay sick before he heard that I was still in the land of the living and a-kicking.

The place on which I lived was sickly and I was determined to leave it. I therefore set out the next fall to look at the country which had been purchased of the Chickasaw tribe of Indians. I went on to a place called Shoal Creek, about eighty miles from where I lived, and here again I got sick. I took the ague and fever, which I supposed was brought on me by camping out. I remained here for some time, as I was unable to go farther; and in that time, I became so well pleased with the country about there, that I resolved to settle in it. It was just only a little distance in the purchase and no order had been established there but I thought I could get along without order as well as any body else. And so I moved and settled myself down on the head of Shoal Creek. We remained here some two or three years, without any law at all, and so many bad characters began to flock in upon us that we found it necessary to set up a sort of temporary government of

our own. I don't mean that we made any president and called him
the "government," but we met and made what we called a corporation; and I reckon we called *it* wrong, for it wa'n't a bank and
hadn't any deposites and now they call the bank a corporation. But
be this as it may, we lived in the back-woods and didn't profess to
know much and no doubt used many wrong words. But we met
and appointed magistrates and constables to keep order. We didn't
fix any laws for them, tho', for we supposed they would know law
enough, whoever they might be, and so we left it to themselves to
fix the laws.

I was appointed one of the magistrates and when a man owed a
debt and wouldn't pay it, I and my constable ordered our warrant
and then he would take the man and bring him before me for trial.
I would give judgment against him and then an order of an execu-
tion would easily scare the debt out of him. If any one was charged
with marking his neighbour's hogs or with stealing anything, which
happened pretty often in those days, I would have him taken and if
there was tolerable grounds for the charge, I would have him well
whip'd and cleared. We kept this up till our Legislature added us to
the white settlements in Giles county and appointed magistrates by
law to organize matters in the parts where I lived. They appointed
nearly every man a magistrate who had belonged to our corporation. I was then, of course, made a squire according to law; though
now the honour rested more heavily on me than before. For, at,
first, whenever I told my constable, says I, "Catch that fellow, and
bring him up for trial" away he went, and the fellow must come,
dead or alive; for we considered this a good warrant, though it was
only in verbal writings. But after I was appointed by the assembly,
they told me my warrants must be in real writing and signed and
that I must keep a book and write my proceedings in it. This was
a hard business on me, for I could just barely write my own name
but to do this, and write the warrants too, was at least a huckle-
berry over my persimmon. I had a pretty well informed constable,
however; and he aided me very much in this business. Indeed I had
so much confidence in him, that I told him, when we should happen to be out anywhere, and see that a warrant was necessary, and

would have a good effect, he need'nt take the trouble to come all the way to me to get one, but he could just fill out one and then on the trial I could correct the whole business if he had committed any error. In this way I got on pretty well, till by care and attention I improved my handwriting in such manner as to be able to prepare my warrants and keep my record book without much difficulty. My judgments were never appealed from and if they had been they would have stuck like wax, as I gave my decisions on the principles of common justice and honesty between man and man and relied on natural born sense, and not on law, learning to guide me, for I had never read a page in a law book in all my life.

CHAPTER 3
Electioneering for the Legislature /
I Make a New Start / A Big Black Bear

About the time we were getting under good headway in our new government, a Capt. Matthews came to me and told me he was a candidate for the office of colonel of a regiment and that I must run for first major in the same regiment. I objected to this, telling him that I thought I had done my share of fighting and that I wanted nothing to do with military appointments.

He still insisted until at last I agreed and of course had every reason to calculate on his support in my election. He was an early settler in that country and made rather more corn than the rest of us and knowing it would afford him a good opportunity to electioneer a little, he made a great corn husking and a great frolic and gave a general treat, asking every body over the whole country. Myself and my family were, of course, invited. When I got there, I found a very large collection of people and some friend of mine soon informed me that the captain's son was going to offer against me for the office of major, which he had seemed so anxious for me to get. I cared nothing about the office, but it put my dander up high enough to see that after he had pressed me so hard to offer, he was countenancing, if not encouraging, a secret plan to beat me. I took the old gentleman out and asked him about it. He told me it was true his son was going to run as a candidate and that he hated worse to run against me than any man in the county. I told him his son need give himself no uneasiness about that; that I shouldn't ran against him for major but against his daddy for colonel. He took me by the hand and we went into the company. He then made a speech and informed the people that I was his opponent. I mounted up for a speech too. I told the people the cause of my opposing him, remarking that as I had the whole family to run against any way, I was determined to levy on the head of the mess. When the time for the election came, his son was opposed by another man for major and he and his daddy were both badly beaten. I just now began to take a rise, as in a little time I was asked to offer for the Legislature in the counties of Lawrence and Heckman.

I offered my name in the month of February and started about the first of March with a drove of horses to the lower part of the state of North Carolina. This was in the year 1821 and I was gone upwards of three months. I returned and set out electioneering, which was a bran-fire new business to me. It now became necessary that I should tell the people something about the government and an eternal sight of other things that I knowed nothing more about than I did about Latin and law and such things as that. I have said before that in those days none of us called Gen'l. Jackson the government, nor did he seem in as fair a way to become so as I do now; but I knowed so little about it, that if any one had told me he was "the government," I should have believed it, for I had never read even a newspaper in my life or any thing else on the subject. But over all my difficulties, it seems to me I was born for luck, though it would be hard for any one to guess what sort. I will, however, explain that hereafter.

I went first into Heckman county to see what I could do among the people as a candidate. Here they told me that they wanted to move their town nearer to the centre of the county, and I must come out in favour of it. There's no devil if I knowed what this meant, or how the town was to be moved; and so I kept dark, going on the identical same plan that I now find is called "non-committal." About this time there was a great squirrel hunt on Duck river, which was among my people. They were to hunt two days: then to meet and count the scalps and have a big barbecue and what might be called a tip-top country frolic. The dinner, and a general treat, was all to be paid for by the party having taken the fewest scalps. I joined one side, taking the place of one of the hunters, and got a gun ready for the hunt. I killed a great many squirrels and when we counted scalps, my party was victorious.

The company had every thing to eat and drink that could be furnished in go new a country, and much fun and good humour prevailed. But before the regular frolic commenced, I mean the dancing, I was called on to make a speech as a candidate; which was a business I was as ignorant of as an outlandish negro.

A public document I had never seen, nor did I know there were such things, and how to begin I couldn't tell. I made many apologies and tried to get off, for I know'd I had a man to run against who could speak prime and I know'd, too, that I wa'n't able to shuffle and cut with him. He was there, and knowing my ignorance as well as I did myself, he also urged me to make a speech. The truth is, he thought my being a candidate was a mere matter of sport and didn't think, for a moment, that he was in any danger from an ignorant back-woods bear hunter. But I found I couldn't get off and so I determined just to go ahead and leave it to chance what I should say. I got up and told the people I reckoned they know'd what I come for, but if not, I could tell them. I had come for their votes and if they didn't watch mighty close, I'd get them too. But the worst of all was that I couldn't tell them any thing about government. I tried to speak about something, and I cared very little

what, until I choaked up as bad as if my mouth had been jam'd and cram'd chock full of dry mush. There the people stood, listening all the while, with their eyes, mouths and ears all open, to catch every word I would speak.

At last I told them I was like a fellow I had heard of not long before. He was beating on the head of an empty barrel near the road-side when a traveler, who was passing along, asked him what he was doing that for? The fellow replied that there was some cider in that barrel a few days before and he was trying to see if there was any then, but if there was he couldn't get at it. I told them that there had been a little bit of a speech in me a while ago but I believed I couldn't get it out. They all roared out in a mighty laugh and I told some other anecdotes, equally amusing to them, believing I had them in a first-rate way, I quit and got down, thanking the people for their attention. But I took care to remark that I was as dry as a powder horn and that I thought it was time for us all to wet our whistles a little and so I put off to the liquor stand and was followed by the greater part of the crowd.

I felt certain this was necessary, for I knowed my competitor could open government matters to them as easy as he pleased. He had, however, mighty few left to hear him, as I continued with the crowd, now and then taking a horn and telling good humoured stories till he was done speaking. I found I was good for the votes at the hunt and when we broke up, I went on to the town of Vernon, which was the same they wanted me to move. Here they pressed me again on the subject and I found I could get either party by agreeing with them. But I told them I didn't know whether it would be right or not and so couldn't promise either way.

Their court commenced on the next Monday, as the barbacue was on a Saturday, and the candidates for governor and for Congress, as well as my competitor and myself, all attended.

The thought of having to make a speech made my knees feel mighty weak and set my heart to fluttering almost as bad as my first love scrape with the Quaker's niece. But as good luck would have it, these big candidates spoke nearly all day and when they quit, the people were worn out with fatigue, which afforded me a good apology for not discussing the government. But I listened mighty close to them and was learning pretty fast about political matters. When they were all done, I got up and told some laughable story and quit. I found I was safe in those parts, and so I went home and didn't go back again till after the election was over. But to cut this matter short, I was elected, doubling my competitor, and nine votes over.

A short time after this, I was in Pulaski where I met with Colonel Polk, now a member of Congress from Tennessee. He was at that time a member elected to the Legislature, as well as myself; and in a large company he said to me, "Well, colonel, I suppose we shall have a radical change of the judiciary at the next session of the Legislature." "Very likely, sir," says I, and I put out quicker, for I was afraid some one would ask me what the judiciary was; and if I knowed I wish I may be shot. I don't indeed believe I had ever before heard that there was any such thing in all nature; but still I was not willing that the people there should know how ignorant I was about it.

When the time for meeting of the Legislature arrived, I went on and before I had been there long, I could have told what the judiciary was and what the government was too, and many other things that I had known nothing about before.

About this time I met with a very severe misfortune, which I may be pardoned for naming, as it made a great change in my circumstances and kept me back very much in the world. I had built an extensive grist mill and powder mill, all connected together, and also a large distillery. They had cost me upwards of three thousand dollars, more than I was worth in the world. The first news that I heard after I got to the Legislature was, that my mills were—not blown up sky high, as you would guess by my powder establishment,—but swept away all to smash by a large fresh that came soon after I left home. I had, of course, to stop my distillery, as my grinding was broken up, and indeed, I may say, that the misfortune just made a complete mash of me. I had some likely negroes and a good stock of almost every thing about me and, best of all, I had an honest wife. She didn't advise me, as is too fashionable, to smuggle up this and that and t'other to go on at home, but she told me, says she, "Just pay up, as long as you have a bit's worth in the world, and then every body will be satisfied and we will scuffle for more." This was just such talk as I wanted to hear, for a man's wife can hold him devlish uneasy, if she begins to scold and fret and perplex him at a time when he has a full load for a rail-road car on his mind already.

And so you see, I determined not to break full handed but thought it better to keep a good conscience with an empty purse than to get a bad opinion of myself with a full one. I therefore gave up all I had and took a bran-fire new start.

* * *

Having returned from the Legislature, I determined to make another move and so I took my eldest son with me and a young man by the name of Abram Henry and cut out for the Obion. I selected a spot when I got there where I determined to settle and the nearest house to it was seven miles, the next nearest was fifteen, and so on to twenty. It was a complete wilderness and full of Indians who were hunting. Game was plenty of almost every kind, which suited me exactly, as I was always fond of hunting. The house which was nearest me and which, as I have already stated, was seven miles off and on the different side of the Obion river, belonged to a man by the name of Owens and I started to go there. I had taken one horse along to pack our provision and when I got to the water I hobbled him out to graze until I got back, as there was no boat to cross the river in and it was so high that it had overflowed all the bottoms and low country near it.

We now took water like so many beavers, notwithstanding it was mighty cold, and waded on. The water would sometimes be up to our necks and at others not so deep but I went, of course, before, and carried a pole with which I would feel along before me to see how deep it was and to guard against falling into a slough, as there was many in our way. When I would come to one, I would take out my tomahawk and cut a small tree across it and then go ahead again. Frequently my little son would have to swim, even where myself and the young man could wade, but we worked on till at last we got to the channel of the river which made it about half a mile we had waded from where we took water. I saw a large tree that had fallen into the river from the other side but it didn't reach across. One stood on the same bank where we were that I thought I could fall so as to reach the other and so at it we went with my tomahawk, cutting away till we got it down and, as good luck would have it, it fell right and made us a way that we could pass.

When we got over this, it was still a sea of water as far as our eyes could reach. We took into it again and went ahead for about a mile, hardly ever seeing a single spot of land, and sometimes very deep. At last we come in sight of land, which was a very pleasing thing and when we got out, we went but a little way before we came in sight of the house, which was more pleasing than ever; for we were wet all over and mighty cold. I felt mighty sorry when I would look at my little boy and see him shaking like he had the worst sort of an ague, for there was no time for fever then. As we got near to the house, we saw Mr. Owens and several men that were with him just starting away. They saw us and stop'd but looked much astonished until we got up to them and I made myself known. The men who were with him were the owners of a boat which was the first that ever went that far up the Obion river, and some hands he had hired to carry it about a hundred miles still further up, by water, tho' it was only about thirty by land, as the river is very crooked.

They all turned back to the house with me, where I found Mrs. Owens, a fine, friendly old woman; and her kindness to my little boy did me ten times as much good as any thing she could have done for me, if she had tried her best. The old gentleman set out his bottle to us and I concluded that if a horn wasn't good then, there was no use for its invention. So I swig'd off about a half pint and the young man was by no means bashful in such a case, he took a strong pull at it too. I then gave my boy some and in a little time we felt pretty well. We dried ourselves by the fire and were asked to go on board of the boat that evening. I agreed to do so, but left my son with the old lady, and myself and my young man went to the boat with Mr. Owens and the others. The boat was loaded with whiskey, flour, sugar, coffee, salt, castings, and other articles suitable for the country; and they were to receive five hundred dollars to land the load at M'Lemore's Bluff, beside the profit they could make on their load. This was merely to show that boats could get up to that point. We stayed all night with them and had a high night of it, as I took steam enough to drive out all the cold that was in me and about three times as much more. In the morning we concluded to go on with the boat to where a great *harricane* had crossed the river and blowed all the timber down into it. When we got there, we found the river was falling fast and concluded we couldn't get through the timber without more rise so we drop'd down opposite Mr. Owens' again, where they determined to wait for more water.

The next day it rained rip-roriously and the river rose pretty considerable, but not enough yet. And so I got the boatsmen all to go out with me to where I was going to settle and we slap'd up a cabin in little or no time. I got from the boat four barrels of meal, one of salt, and about ten gallons of whiskey.

To pay for these, I agreed to go with the boat up the river to their landing place. I got also a large middling of bacon and killed a fine deer and left them for my young man and my little boy, who were to stay at my cabin till I got back, which I expected would be in six or seven days. We cut out and moved up to the harricane, where we stop'd for the night. In the morning I started about daylight, intending to kill a deer, as I had no thought they would get the boat through the timber that day. I had gone but a little way before I killed a fine buck and started to go back to the boat but on the way I came on the tracks of a large gang of elks and so I took after them. I had followed them only a little distance when I saw them and directly after I saw two large bucks. I shot one down and the other wouldn't leave him so I loaded my gun and shot him down too. I hung them up and went ahead again after my elks. I pursued on till after the middle of the day before I saw them again, but they took the hint before I got in shooting distance and ran off. I still pushed on till late in the evening when I found I was about four miles from where I had left the boat and as hungry as a wolf, for I hadn't eaten a bite that day.

I started down the edge of the river low grounds, giving out the pursuit of my elks, and hadn't gone hardly any distance at all before I saw two more bucks, very large fellows too. I took a blizzard at one of them and up he tumbled. The other ran off a few jumps and stop'd and stood there till I loaded again to fire at him. I knock'd his trotters from under him and then I hung them both up. I pushed on again and about sunset I saw three other bucks. I down'd with one of them and the other two ran off. I hung this one up also, having now killed six that day. I then pushed on till I got to the harricane, and at the lower edge of it, about where I expected the boat was. Here I hollered as hard as I could roar, but could get no answer. I fired off my gun and the men on the boat fired one too, but quite contrary to my expectation, they had got through the timber and were about two miles above me. It was now dark and I had to crawl through the fallen timber the best way I could; and if the reader don't know it was bad enough, I am sure I do. For the vines and briers had grown all through it and so thick that a good fat coon couldn't much more than get along. I got through at last and went on near to where I had killed my last deer and once more fired off my gun, which was again answered from the boat, which was still a little above me. I moved on as fast as I could, but soon came to water, and not knowing how deep it was, I halted and hollered till they came to me with a skiff. I now got to the boat without further difficulty but the briers had worked on me at such a rate that I felt like I wanted sewing up all over. I took a pretty stiff horn, which soon made me feel much better, but I was so tired that I could hardly work my jaws to eat.

In the morning, myself and a young man started and brought in the first buck I had killed and after breakfast we went and brought in the last one. The boat then started, but we again went and got the two I had killed just as I turned down the river in the evening; and we then pushed on and o'ertook the boat, leaving the other two hanging in the woods, as we had now as much as we wanted.

We got up the river very well, but quite slowly, and we landed on the eleventh day at the place the load was to be delivered at. They here gave me their skiff and myself and a young man by the name of Flavins Harris, who had determined to go and live with me, cut out down the river for my cabin, which we reached safely enough.

We turned in and cleared a field and planted our corn but it was so late in the spring, we had no time to make rails and therefore we put no fence around our field. There was no stock, however, nor any thing else to disturb our corn, except the wild *varments* and the old serpent himself, with a fence to help him, couldn't keep them out. I made corn enough to do me, and during that spring I killed ten bears and a great abundance of deer. But in all this time, we saw the face of no white person in that country, except Mr. Owens' family and a very few passengers who went out there, looking at the country. Indians, though, were still plenty enough. Having laid by my crap, I went home, which was a distance of about a hundred and fifty miles and when I got there, I was met by an order to attend a call-session of our Legislature. I attended it and served out my time and then returned and took my family and what little plunder I had, and moved to where I had built my cabin and made my crap.

I gathered my corn and then set out for my Fall's hunt. This was in the last of October, 1822. I found bear very plenty and, indeed, all sorts of game and wild varments, except buffalo. There was none of them. I hunted on till Christmass, having supplied my family very well all along with wild meat, at which time my powder gave out and I had none either to fire Christmass guns, which is very common in that country, or to hunt with. I had a brother-in-law who had now moved out and settled about six miles west of me, on the opposite side of Rutherford's fork of the Obion river, and he had brought me a keg of powder, but I had never gotten it home. There had just been another of Noah's freshes and the low grounds were flooded all over with water. I know'd the stream was at least a mile wide which I would have to cross, as the water was from hill to hill, and yet I determined to go on over in some way or other, so as to get my powder. I told this to my wife and she immediately opposed it with all her might. I still insisted, telling her we had no powder for Christmass and, worse than all, we were out of meat. She said we had as well starve as for me to freeze to death or to get drowned, one or the other was certain if I attempted to go.

But I didn't believe the half of this and so I took my woolen wrappers and a pair of mockasins and put them on and tied up some dry clothes and a pair of shoes and stockings and started. But I didn't before know how much any body could suffer and not die. This, and some of my other experiments in water, learned me something about it and I therefore relate them.

The snow was about four inches deep when I started and when I got to the water, which was only about a quarter of a mile off, it look'd like an ocean. I put in and waded on till I come to the channel where I crossed that on a high log. I then took water again, having my gun and all my hunting tools along, and waded till I came to a deep slough that was wider than the river itself. I had crossed it often on a log but, behold, when I got there, no log was to be seen. I knowed of an island in the slough and a sapling stood on it close to the side of that log, which was now entirely under water. I knowed further that the water was about eight or ten feet deep under the log and I judged it to be about three feet deep over it. After studying a little what I should do, I determined to cut a forked sapling, which stood near me, so as to lodge it against the one that stood on the island, in which I succeeded very well. I then cut me a pole and crawled along on my sapling till I got to the one it was lodged against which was about six feet above the water. I then felt about with my pole till I found the log which was just about as deep under the water as I had judged. I then crawled back and got my gun, which I had left at the stump of the sapling I had cut and again made my way to the place of lodgement and then climb'd down the other sapling so as to get on the log. I then felt my way along with my feet, in the water about waist deep, but it was a mighty ticklish business. However, I got over and by this time I had very little feeling in my feet and legs as I had been all the time in the water, except what time I was crossing the high log over the river, and climbing my lodged sapling.

I went but a short distance before I came to another slough, over which there was a log, but it was floating on the water. I thought I could walk it and so I mounted on it but when I had got about the middle of the deep water somehow, it turned over and in I went up to my head I waded out of this deep water, and went ahead till I came to the high-land, where I stop'd to pull off my wet clothes and put on the others, which I had held up with my gun, above the water, when I fell in. I got them on but my flesh had no feeling in it, I was so cold. I tied up the wet ones and hung them up in a bush. I now thought I would run so as to warm myself a little, but I couldn't raise a trot for some time. Indeed, I couldn't step more than half the length of my foot. After a while I got better and went on five miles to the house of my brother-in-law, having not even smelt fire from the time I started. I got there late in the evening and he was much astonished at seeing me at such a time. I stayed all night and the next morning was most piercing cold, so they persuaded me not to go home that day. I agreed and turned out and killed him two deer, but the weather still got worse and colder, instead of better. I stayed that night and in the morning they still insisted I couldn't get home. I knowed the water would be frozen over but not hard enough to bear me, so I agreed to stay that day. I went out hunting again and pursued a big *he-bear* all day, but didn't kill him. The next morning was bitter cold but I knowed my family was without meat and I determined to get home to them or die a-trying.

I took my keg of powder and all my hunting tools and cut out. When I got to the water, it was a sheet of ice as far as I could see. I put on to it, but hadn't got far before it broke through with me and so I took out my tomahawk and broke my way along before me for a considerable distance. At last I got to where the ice would bear me for a short distance and I mounted on it and went ahead but it soon broke in again and I had to wade on till I

came to my floating log. I found it so tight this time that I know'd it couldn't give me another fall as it was frozen in with the ice. I crossed over it without much difficulty and worked along till I got to my lodged sapling and my log under the water. The swiftness of the current prevented the water from freezing over it and so I had to wade, just as I did when I crossed it before. When I got to my sapling, I left my gun and climbed out with my powder keg first and then went back and got my gun. By this time I was nearly frozen to death but I saw all along before me, where the ice had been fresh broke, and I thought it must be a bear straggling about in the water. I, therefore, fresh primed my gun and, cold as I was, I was determined to make war on him if we met. But I followed the trail till it led me home and I then found it had been made by my young man that lived with me who had been sent by my distressed wife to see, if he could, what had become of me, for they all believed that I was dead. When I got home I was'nt quite dead but mighty nigh it; I had my powder and that was what I went for.

* * *

THAT night there fell a heavy rain and it turned to a sleet. In the morning all hands turned out hunting. My young man and a brother-in-law who had lately settled close by me, went down the river to hunt for turkeys but I was for larger game. I told them I had dreamed the night before of having a hard fight with a big black nigger and I knowed it was a sign that I was to have a battle with a bear for in a bear country, I never know'd such a dream to fail. So I started to go up above the harricane, determined to have a bear. I had two pretty good dogs and an old hound, all of which I took along. I had gone about six miles up the river and it was then about four miles across to the main Obion, so I determined to strike across to that, as I had found nothing yet to kill. I got on to the river and turned down it, but the sleet was still getting worse and worse. The bushes were all bent down and locked together with ice so that it was almost impossible to get along. In a little time my dogs started a large gang of old turkey goblers and I killed two of them, of the biggest sort. I shouldered them up and moved on, until I got through the harricane, when I was so tired that I laid my goblers down to rest, as they were confounded heavy and I was mighty tired. While I was resting, my old hound went to a log and smelt it awhile and then raised his eyes toward the sky and cried out. Away he went, and my other dogs with him, and I shouldered up my turkeys again and followed on as hard as I could drive. They were soon out of sight and in a very little time I heard them begin to bark. When I got to them, they were barking up a

tree, but there was no game there. I concluded it had been a turkey and that it had flew away.

When they saw me coming, away they went again and, after a little time, began to bark as before. When I got near them, I found they were barking up the wrong tree again, as there was no game there. They served me in this way three or four times until I was so infernal mad that I determined, if I could get near enough, to shoot the old hound at least. With this intention I pushed on harder till I came to the edge of an open parara. Looking on before my dogs, I saw in and about the biggest bear that ever was seen in America. He looked, at the distance he was from me, like a large black bull. My dogs were afraid to attack him and that was the reason they had stop'd so often, that I might overtake them. They were now almost up with him and I took my goblers from my back and hung them up in a sapling and broke like a quarter horse after my bear, for the sight of him had put new springs in me. I soon got near to them but they were just getting into a roaring thicket and so I couldn't run through it, but had to pick my way along and had close work even at that.

In a little time I saw the bear climbing up a large black oak-tree and I crawled on till I got within about eighty yards of him. He was setting with his breast to me and so I put fresh priming in my gun and fired at him. At this he raised one of his paws and snorted loudly. I loaded again as quick as I could and fired as near the same place in his breast as possible. At the crack of my gun here he came tumbling down and the moment he touched the ground I heard one of my best dogs cry out. I took my tomahawk in one hand and my big butcher-knife in the other, and run up within four or five paces of him, at which he let my dog go and fixed his eyes on me. I got back in all sorts of a hurry, for I know'd if he got hold of me, he would hug me altogether too close for comfort. I went to my gun and hastily loaded her again and shot him the third time, which killed him good.

I now began to think about getting him home, but I didn't know how far it was. So I left him and started and in order to find him again, I would blaze a sapling every little distance, which would

show me the way back. I continued this till I got within about a
mile of home, for there I know'd very well where I was, and that I
could easily find the way back to my blazes. When I got home, I
took my brother-in-law and my young man and four horses and
went back. We got there just before dark and struck up a fire and
commenced butchering my bear. It was some time in the night
before we finished it; and I can assert, on my honour, that I believe
he would have weighed six hundred pounds. It was the second
largest I ever saw. I killed one, a few years after, that weighed six

hundred and seventeen pounds. I now felt fully compensated for my sufferings in going after my powder and well satisfied that a dog might sometimes be doing a good business, even when he seemed to be barking up the wrong tree. We got our meat home and I had the pleasure to know that we now had plenty and that of the best and I continued through the winter to supply my family abundantly with bear-meat and venison from the woods.

Chapter 4
I Stand for the Federal Congress / More Hunting Adventures / Down the Mississippi / Elected to Congress

I had on hand a great many skins and so, in the month of February, I packed a horse with them and taking my eldest son along with me, cut out for a little town called Jackson, situated about forty miles off. We got there well enough and I sold my skins and bought me some coffee and sugar, powder, lead and salt. I packed them all up in readiness for a start, which I intended to make early the next morning. Morning came but I concluded, before I started, I would go and take a horn with some of my old fellow-soldiers that I had met with at Jackson.

I did so and while we were engaged in this, I met with three candidates for the Legislature; a Doctor Butler, who was, by marriage, a nephew to General Jackson, a Major Lynn, and a Mr. McEver, all first-rate men. We all took a horn together and some person present said to me, "Crockett, you must offer for the Legislature." I told him I lived at least forty miles from any white settlement and had no thought of becoming a candidate at that time. So we all parted and I and my little boy went on home.

It was about a week or two after this that a man came to my house and told me I was a candidate. I told him not so. But he took out a newspaper from his pocket and showe'd me where I was announced. I said to my wife that this was all a burlesque on me, but I was determined to make it cost the man who had put it there at least the value of the printing and of the fun he wanted at my expense. So I hired a young man to work in my place on my farm and turned out myself electioneering. I hadn't been out long before I found the people began to talk very much about the bear hunter, the man from the cane and the three gentlemen, who I have already named, soon found it necessary to enter into an agreement to have a sort of caucus at their March court to determine which of them was the strongest and the other two was to withdraw and support him. As the court came on, each one of them spread himself to secure the nomination but it fell on Dr. Butler and the rest backed out. The doctor was a clever fellow and I have often said he was the most talented man I ever run against for any office. His being related to Gen'l. Jackson also helped him on very much but I was in for it and I was determined to push ahead and go through or stick. Their meeting was held in Madison county, which was the strongest in the representative district and composed of eleven counties that seemed bent on having the member from there.

At this time Col. Alexander was a candidate for Congress and attending one of his public meetings one day, I walked to where he was treating the people and he gave me an introduction to several of his acquaintances and informed them that I was out electioneering.

In a little time my competitor, Doctor Butler, came along. He passed by without noticing me and I suppose, indeed, he did not recognise me. But I hailed him, as I was for all sorts of fun, and when he turned to me, I said to him, "Well, doctor, I suppose they have weighed you out to me; but I should like to know why they fixed your election for *March* instead of *August?* This is," said I, "a branfire new way of doing business, if a caucus is to make a representative for the people!" He now discovered who I was, and cried out, "D——n it, Crockett, is that you?" "Be sure it is," said I, "but I don't want it understood that I have come electioneering. I have just crept out of the cane to see what discoveries I could make among the white folks." I told him that when I set out electioneering, I would go prepared to put every man on as good footing when I left him as I found him. I would therefore have me a large buckskin hunting-shirt made with a couple of pockets holding about a peck each and that in one I would carry a great big twist of tobacco and in the other my bottle of liquor, for I knowed when I met a man and offered him a dram, he would throw out his quid of tobacco to take one and after he had taken his horn, I would go out with my twist and give him another chaw. And in this way he would not be worse off than when I found him and I would be sure to leave him in a first-rate good humour. He said I could beat him electioneering all hollow. I told him I would give him better evidence of that before August, notwithstanding he had many advantages over me, particularly in the way of money, but I told him that I would go on the products of the country, that I had industrious children and the best of coon dogs and they would hunt every night till midnight to support my election and when the coon fur wa'n't good, I would myself go a wolfing and shoot down a wolf, skin his head and his scalp would be good to me for three dollars in our state treasury money; and in this way I would get along on the big string. He stood like he was both amused and astonished and the whole crowd was in a roar of laughter. From this place I returned home, leaving the people in a first-rate way and I was sure I would do a good business among them. At any rate, I was determined to stand up to my lick-log, salt or no salt.

In a short time there came out two other candidates, a Mr. Shaw and a Mr. Brown. We all ran the race through and when the election was over, it turned out that I beat them all by a majority of two hundred and forty-seven votes and was again returned as a member of the Legislature from a new region of the country without losing a session. This reminded me of the old saying "A fool for luck, and a poor man for children."

I now served two years in that body from my new district, which was the years 1823 and '24. At the session of 1823, I had a small trial of my independence and whether I would forsake principle for party or for the purpose of following after big men.

The term of Col. John Williams had expired, who was a senator in Congress from the state of Tennessee. He was a candidate for another election and was opposed by Pleasant M. Miller, Esq., who, it was believed, would not be able to beat the colonel. Some two or three others were spoken of, but it was at last concluded that the only man who could beat him was the present "government," General Jackson. So, a few days before the election was to come on, he was sent for to come and run for the senate. He was then in nomination for the presidency but sure-enough he came and did run as the opponent of

Colonel Williams, and beat him too, but not by my vote. The vote was for Jackson *thirty-five;* for Williams, *twenty-five.* I thought the colonel had honestly discharged his duty and even the mighty name of Jackson couldn't make me vote against him.

But voting against the old chief was found a mighty up-hill business to all of them except myself. I never would, nor never did, acknowledge I had voted wrong and I am more certain now that I was right than ever.

I told the people it was the best vote I ever gave; that I had supported the public interest and cleared my conscience in giving it, instead of gratifying the private ambition of a man.

I let the people know as early as then that I wouldn't take a collar around my neck with the letters engraved on it:

MY DOG.

ANDREW JACKSON.

During these two sessions of the Legislature, nothing else turned up which I think it worth while to mention and indeed, I am fearful that I am too particular about many small matters but if so, my apology is that I want the world to understand my true history and how I worked along to rise from a cane-brake to my present station in life.

Col. Alexander was the representative in Congress of the district I lived in and his vote on the tariff law of 1824 gave a mighty heap of dissatisfaction to his people. They therefore began to talk pretty strong of running me for Congress against him. At last I was called on by a good many to be a candidate. I told the people that I couldn't stand that; it was a step above my knowledge and I know'd nothing about Congress.

However, I was obliged to agree to run and myself and two other gentlemen came out. But Providence was a little against two of us this hunt, for it was the year that cotton brought twenty-five dollars a hundred; and so Colonel Alexander would get up and tell the people, it was all the good effect of this tariff law; that it had raised the price of their cotton and that it would raise the price of

every thing else they made to sell. I might as well have sung *Psalms* over a dead horse as to try to make the people believe otherwise, for they knowed their cotton had raised, sure enough, and if the colonel hadn't done it, they didn't know what had. So he rather made a mash of me this time, as he beat me exactly *two* votes, as they counted the polls, though I have always believed that many other things had been as fairly done as that same count.

He went on and served out his term and at the end of it, cotton was down to *six* or *eight* dollars a hundred again and I concluded I would try him once more and see how it would go with cotton at the common price and so I became a candidate.

* * *

BUT the reader, I expect, would have no objection to know a little about my employment during the two years while my competitor was in Congress. In this space I had some pretty tuff times and will relate some few things that happened to me. So here goes, as the boy said when he run by himself.

In the fall of 1825, I concluded I would build two large boats and load them with pipe staves for market. So I went down to the lake, which was about twenty-five miles from where I lived, and hired some hands to assist me and went to work; some at boat building, and others to getting slaves. I worked on with my hands till the bears got fat and then I turned out to hunting, to lay in a supply of meat. I soon killed and salted down as many as were necessary for my family; but about this time one of my old neighbours, who had settled down on the lake about twenty-five miles from me, came to my house and told me he wanted me to go down and kill some bears about in his parts. He said they were extremely fat and very plenty. I know'd that when they were fat, they were easily taken, for a fat bear can't run fast or long. But I asked a bear no favours, no way, further than civility, for I now had *eight* large dogs, and as fierce as painters, so that a bear stood no chance at all to get away from them. So I went home with him and then went on down towards the Mississippi and commenced hunting.

We were out two weeks and in that time killed fifteen bears. Having now supplied my friend with plenty of meat, I engaged occasionally again with my hands in our boat building and getting slaves. But I at length couldn't stand it any longer without another hunt. So I concluded to take my little son and cross over the lake and take a hunt there. We got over and that evening turned out and killed three bears in little or no time. The next morning we drove up four forks and made a sort of scaffold on which we salted up our meat so as to have it out of the reach of the wolves, for as soon as we would leave our camp, they would take possession. We had just eaten our breakfast when a company of hunters came to our camp, they had fourteen dogs but all so poor that when they would bark they would almost have to lean up against a tree and take a rest. I told them their dogs couldn't run in smell of a bear and they had better stay at my camp and feed them on the bones I had cut out of my meat. I left them there and cut out but I hadn't gone far when my dogs took a first-rate start after a very large fat old *he-bear,* which run right plump towards my camp. I pursued on, but my other hunters had heard my dogs coming and met them and killed the bear before I got up with him. I gave him to them and cut out again for a creek called Big Clover, which wa'n't very far off. Just as I got there, and was entering a cane brake, my dogs all broke and went ahead and, in a little time, they raised a fuss in the cane and seemed to be going every way. I listened a while and found my dogs in two companies and that both was in a snorting fight. I sent my little son to one and I broke for t'other. I got to mine first and found my dogs had a two-year-old bear down, a-wooling away on him, so I just took out my big butcher and went up and slap'd it into him, killing him without shooting. There was five of the dogs in my company. In a short time, I heard my little son fire at his bear; when I went to him he had killed it too. He had two dogs in his team. Just at this moment we heard my other dog barking a short distance off and all the rest immediately broke to him. We pushed on too, and when we got there, we found he had still a larger bear than either of them we had killed, treed by himself. We killed that one also, which made three we had killed in less than half an hour. We turned in and butchered them and then started to hunt for water and a good place to camp. But we had no sooner started, than our dogs took a start after another one and away they went like a thunder-gust and was out of hearing in a minute. We followed the way they had gone for some time, but at length we gave up the hope of finding them and turned back. As we were going back, I came to where a poor fellow was grubbing and he looked like the very picture of hard times. I asked him what he was doing away there in the woods by himself? He said he was grubbing for a man who intended to settle there and the reason why he did it was that he had no meat for his family and he was working for a little.

I was mighty sorry for the poor fellow, for it was not only a hard, but a very slow way to get meat for a hungry family, so I told him if he would go with me, I would give him more meat than he could get by grubbing in a month. I intended to supply him with meat and also to get him to assist my little boy in packing in and salting up my bears. He had never seen a bear killed in his life. I told him I had six killed then and my dogs were hard after another. He went off to his little cabin, which was a short distance in the brush, and his wife was very anxious he should go with me. So we started and went to where I had left my three bears and made a camp. We then gathered my meat and salted and scaffled it, as I had done with the other. Night now came on but no word from my dogs yet. I afterwards found they had treed the bear about five miles off, near to a man's house, and had barked at it the whole enduring night. Poor fellows! Many a time they looked for me and wondered why I didn't come, for they knowed there was no mistake in me and I know'd they were as good as ever fluttered. In the morning, as soon as it was light enough to see, the man took his gun and went to them, and shot

the bear and killed it. My dogs, however, wouldn't have any thing to say to this stranger; so they left him and came early in the morning back to me.

We got our breakfast and cut out again and we killed four large and very fat bears that day. We hunted out the week and in that time we killed seventeen, all of them first-rate. When we closed our hunt, I gave the man over a thousand weight of fine fat bear-meat, which pleased him mightily and made him feel as rich as a Jew. I saw him the next fall and he told me he had plenty of meat to do him the whole year from his week's hunt. My son and me now went home. This was the week between Christmass and New-year that we made this hunt.

When I got home, one of my neighbours was out of meat and wanted me to go back and let him go with me to take another hunt. I couldn't refuse but I told him I was afraid the bear had taken to house by that time, for after they get very fat in the fall and early part of the winter, they go into their holes in large hollow trees or into hollow logs, or their cane-houses, or the harricanes, and lie there till spring like frozen snakes. And one thing about this will seem mighty strange to many people. From about the first of January to about the last of April, these varments lie in their holes altogether. In all that time they have no food to eat and yet when they come out, they are not an ounce lighter than when they went to house. I don't know the cause of this, and still I know it is a fact, and I leave it for others who have more learning than myself to account for it. They have not a particle of food with them, but they just lie and suck the bottom of their paw all the time. I have killed many of them in their trees, which enables me to speak positively on this subject. However, my neighbour, whose name was McDaniel, and my little son and me, went on down to the lake to my second camp, where I had killed my seventeen bears the week before, and turned out to hunting. But we hunted hard all day without getting a single start. We had carried but little provisions with us, and the next morning was entirely out of meat I sent my son about three miles off to the house of an old friend to get some. The old gentleman was much pleased to hear I was hunting in those parts, for the year before the bears had killed a great many of his hogs. He was that day killing his bacon hogs, and so he gave my son some meat and sent word to me that I must come in to his house that evening, that he would have plenty of feed for my dogs and some accommodations for ourselves but before my son got back, we had gone out hunting and in a large cane brake my dogs found a big bear in a cane-house, which he had fixed for his winter-quarters, as they sometimes do.

When my lead dog found him, and raised the yell, all the rest broke to him but none of them entered his house until we got up. I encouraged my dogs, and they knowed me so well that I could have made them seize the old serpent himself, with all his horns and heads and cloven foot and ugliness into the bargain, if he would only have come to light, so that they could have seen him. They bulged in and in an instant the bear followed them out and I told my friend to shoot him as he was mighty wrathy to kill a bear. He did so and killed him prime. We carried him to our camp, by which time my son had returned, and after we got our dinners we packed up, and cut for the house of my old friend, whose name was Davidson.

We got there and staid with him that night and the next morning, having salted up our meat, we left it with him and started to take a hunt between the Obion lake and the Red-foot lake; as there had been a dreadful harricane, which passed between them,

and I was sure there must be a heap of bears in the fallen timber. We had gone about five miles without seeing any sign at all but at length we got on some high cany ridges and, as we rode along, I saw a hole in a large black oak and on examining more closely, I discovered that a bear had climbed the tree. I could see his tracks going up, but none coming down, and so I was sure he was in there. A person who is acquainted with bear-hunting can tell easy enough when the varment is in the hollow, for as they go up they don't slip a bit, but as they come down they make long scratches with their nails.

My friend was a little ahead of me but I called him back and told him there was a bear in that tree and I must have him out. So we lit from our horses and I found a small tree which I thought I could fall so as to lodge against my bear tree and we fell to work chopping it with our tomahawks. I intended, when we lodged the tree against the other, to let my little son go up and look into the hole, for he could climb like a squirrel. We had chop'd on a little time and stop'd to rest when I heard my dogs barking mighty severe at some distance from us and I told my friend I knowed they had a bear; for it is the nature of a dog, when he finds you are hunting bears, to hunt for nothing else; he becomes fond of the meat, and considers other game as "not worth a notice," as old Johnson said of the devil.

We concluded to leave our tree a bit and went to my dogs and when we got there, sure enough they had an eternal great big fat bear up a tree, just ready for shooting. My friend again petitioned me for liberty to shoot this one also. I had a little rather not, as the bear was so big, but I came the old fellow like some great log had fell. I now missed one of my dogs, the same that I before spoke of as having treed the bear by himself sometime before, when I had started the three in the cane break. I told my friend that my missing dog had a bear somewhere, just as sure as fate, so I left them to butcher the one we had just killed and I went up on a piece of high ground to listen for my dog. I heard him barking with all his might some distance off and I pushed ahead for him. My other dogs hearing him broke to him, and when I got there, sure enough again he had another bear ready treed; if he hadn't, I wish I may be shot. I fired on him and brought him down and then went back and help'd finish butchering the one at which I had left my friend. We then packed both to our tree where we had left my boy. By this time, the little fellow had cut the tree down that we intended to lodge but it fell the wrong way; he had then feather'd in on the big tree, to cut that, and had found that it was nothing but a shell on the outside, and all doted in the middle, as too many of our big men are in these days having only an outside appearance. My friend and my son cut away on it and I went off about a hundred yards with my dogs to keep them from running under the tree when it should fall. On looking back at the hole, I saw the bear's head out of it, looking down at them as they were cutting. I hollered to them to look up, and they did so; and McDaniel catched up his gun, but by this time the bear was out and coming down the tree. He fired at it, and as soon as it touch'd ground the dogs were all round it. They had a roll-and-tumble fight to the foot of the hill, where they stop'd him. I ran up, and putting my gun against the bear, fired and killed him. We now had three, and so we made our scaffold and salted them up.

* * *

In the morning I left my son at the camp, and we started on towards
the harricane; and when we had went about a mile, we started a
very large bear, but we got along mighty slow on account of the
cracks in the earth occasioned by the earthquakes. We, however,
made out to keep in hearing of the dogs for about three miles, and
then we come to the harricane. Here we had to quit our horses,
as old Nick himself couldn't have got through it without sneak-
ing it along in the form that he put on, to make a fool of our old
grandmother Eve. By this time several of my dogs had got tired
and come back; but we went ahead on foot for some little time
in the harricane when we met a bear coming straight to us, and
not more than twenty or thirty yards off. I started my tired dogs
after him and McDaniel pursued them and I went on to where my

other dogs were. I had seen the track of the bear they were after and I knowed he was a screamer. I followed on to about the middle of the harricane but my dogs pursued him so close that they made him climb an old stump about twenty feet high. I got in shooting distance of him and fired, but I was all over in such a flutter from fatigue and running, that I couldn't hold steady; but, however, I broke his shoulder and he fell. I run up and loaded my gun as quick as possible and shot him again and killed him. When I went to take out my knife to butcher him, I found I had lost it in coming through the harricane. The vines and briers was so thick that I would sometimes have to get down and crawl like a varment to get through at all; and a vine had, as I supposed, caught in the handle and pulled it out. While I was standing and studying what to do, my friend came to me. He had followed my trail through the harricane and had found my knife, which was mighty good news to me; as a hunter hates the worst in the world to lose a good dog or any part of his hunting-tools. I now left McDaniel to butcher the bear and I went after our horses and brought them as near as the nature of case would allow. I then took our bags and went back to where he was and when we had skin'd the bear, we fleeced off the fat and carried it to our horses at several loads. We then packed it up on our horses and had a heavy pack of it on each one. We now started and went on till about sunset, when I concluded we must be near our camp, so I hollered and my son answered me and we moved on in the direction to the camp. We had gone but a little way when I heard my dogs make a warm start again and I jumped down from my horse and gave him up to my friend and told him I would follow them. He went on to the camp and I went ahead after my dogs with all my might for a considerable distance, till at last night came on. The woods were very rough and hilly and all covered over with cane.

I now was compel'd to move on more slowly and was frequently falling over logs and into the cracks made by the earthquakes so that I was very much afraid I would break my gun. However I went on about three miles when I came to a good big creek, which I waded. It was very cold, the creek was about knee-deep, but I felt no great inconvenience from it just then, as I was all over wet with sweat from running and I felt hot enough. After I got over this creek and out of the cane, which was very thick on all our creeks, I listened for my dogs. I found they had either treed or brought the bear to a stop, as they continued barking in the same place. I pushed on as near in the direction to the noise as I could, till I found the hill was too steep for me to climb, and so I backed and went down the creek some distance till I came to a hollow, and then took up that, till I come to a place where I could climb up the hill. It was mighty dark and was difficult to see my way or any thing else. When I got up the hill, I found I had passed the dogs so I turned and went to them. I found, when I got there, they had treed the bear in a large forked poplar and it was setting in the fork.

I could see the lump, but not plain enough to shoot with any certainty, as there was no moonlight and so I set in to hunting for some dry brush to make me a light; but I could find none, though I could find that the ground was torn mightily to pieces by the cracks.

At last I thought I could shoot by guess and kill him, so I pointed as near the lump as I could, and fired away. But the bear didn't come he only climbed up higher and got out on a limb, which helped me to see him better. I now loaded up again and fired, but this time he didn't move at all. I commenced loading for a third fire, but the first thing I knowed, the bear was down among my dogs and they were fighting all around me I had my big butcher in my belt and I had a pair of dressed buckskin breeches on. So I took out my knife and stood, determined, if he should get hold of me, to defend myself in the best way I could. I stood there for some time, and could now and then see a white dog I had, but the rest of them, and the bear, which were dark coloured, I couldn't see at all, it was so miserable dark. They still fought around me, and sometimes within three feet of me but, at last, the bear got down into one of the cracks, that the earthquakes had made in the ground, about four feet deep, and I could tell the biting end of him by the hollering of my dogs. So I took my gun and pushed the muzzle of it about till I thought I had it against the main part of his body, and fired; but it happened to be only the fleshy part of his foreleg. With this, he jumped out of the crack, and he and the dogs had another hard fight around me, as before. At last, however, they forced him back into the crack again, as he was when I had shot.

I had laid down my gun in the dark, and I now began to hunt for it and, while hunting, I got hold of a pole and I concluded I would punch him awhile with that. I did so, and when I would punch him, the dogs would jump in on him, when he would bite them badly and they would jump out again. I concluded, as he would take punching so patiently, it might be that he would lie still enough for me to get down in the crack, and feel slowly along till I could find the right place to give him a dig with my butcher. So I got down, and my dogs got in before him and kept his head towards them, till I got along easily up to him. Placing my hand on his rump, I felt for his shoulder, just behind which I intended to stick him. I made a lounge with my long knife, and fortunately stuck him right through the heart, at which he just sank down and I crawled out in a hurry. In a little time my dogs all come out too and seemed satisfied, which was the way they always had of telling me that they had finished him.

I suffered very much that night with cold, as my leather breeches, and every thing else I had on, was wet and frozen. But I managed to get my bear out of this crack after several hard trials, and so I butchered him, and laid down to try to sleep. But my fire was very bad and I couldn't find any thing that would burn well to make it any better and I concluded I should freeze, if I didn't warm myself in some way by exercise. So I got up, and hollered a while, and then I would just jump up and down with all my might and throw myself into all sorts of motions. But all this wouldn't do; for my blood was now getting cold and the chills coming all over me. I was so tired, too, that I could hardly walk but I thought I would do the best I could to save my life, and then, if I died, nobody would be to blame. So I went to a tree about two feet through and not a limb on it for thirty feet and I would climb up it to the limbs and then lock my arms together around it and slide down to the bottom again. This would make the insides of my legs and arms feel mighty warm and good. I continued this till daylight in the morning. How often

I climb up my tree and slid down I don't know, but I reckon at least a hundred times.

In the morning I got my bear hung up so as to be safe and then set out to hunt for my camp. I found it after a while and McDaniel and my son were very much rejoiced to see me get back, for they were about to give me up for lost. We got our breakfasts and then secured our meat by building a high scaffold and covering it over. We had no fear of its spoiling, for the weather was so cold that it couldn't.

We now started after my other bear, which had caused me so much trouble and suffering and before we got him, we got a start after another and took him also. We went on to the creek I had crossed the night before and camped, and then went to where my bear was, that I had killed in the crack. When we examined the place, McDaniel said he wouldn't have gone into it, as I did, for all the bears in the woods.

We took the meat down to our camp and salted it and also the last one we had killed, intending, in the morning, to make a hunt in the harricane again.

We prepared for resting that night and I can assure the reader I was in need of it. We had laid down by our fire, and about ten o'clock there came a most terrible earthquake, which shook the earth so that we were rocked about like we had been in a cradle. We were very much alarmed, for though we were accustomed to feel earthquakes, we were now right in the region which had been torn to pieces by them in 1812 and we thought it might take a notion and swallow us up, like the big fish did Jonah.

In the morning we packed up and moved to the harricane, where we made another camp and turned out that evening and killed a very large bear, which made *eight* we had now killed in this hunt.

The next morning we entered the harricane again and in little or no time my dogs were in full cry. We pursued them and soon came to a thick cane-brake, in which they had stop'd their bear. We got up close to him, as the cane was so thick that we couldn't see more than a few feet. Here I made my friend hold the cane a little open with his gun till I shot the bear, which was a mighty large one.

I killed him dead in his tracks. We got him out and butchered him and in a little time started another and killed him, which now made *ten* we had killed and we know'd we couldn't pack any more home, as we had only five horses along. Therefore we returned to the camp and salted up all our meat to be ready for a start homeward next morning.

The morning came and we packed our horses with the meat and had as much as they could possibly carry and sure enough cut out for home. It was about thirty miles and we reached home the second day. I had now accommodated my neighbour with meat enough to do him, and had killed in all, up to that time, fifty-eight bears during the fall and winter.

As soon as the time come for them to quit their houses and come out again in the spring. I took a notion to hunt a little more and in about one month I killed forty-seven more, which made one hundred and five bears I had killed in less than one year from that time.

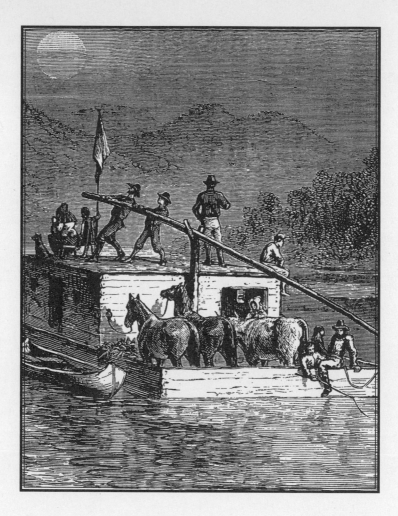

* * *

HAVING now closed my hunting for that winter, I returned to my hands, who were engaged about my boats and staves, and made ready for a trip down the river. I had two boats and about thirty thousand staves and so I loaded with them and set out for

New Orleans. I got out of the Obion river, in which I had loaded my boats, very well; but when I got into the Mississippi, I found all my hands were bad scared and in fact I believe I was scared a little the worst of any; for I had never been down the river and I soon discovered that my pilot was as ignorant of the business as myself. I hadn't gone far before I determined to lash the two boats together; we did so, but it made them so heavy and obstinate that it was next akin to impossible to do any thing at all with them or to guide them right in the river.

That evening we fell in company with some Ohio boats and about night we tried to land, but we could not. The Ohio men hollered to us to go on and run all night. We took their advice, though we had a good deal rather not but we couldn't do any other way. In a short distance we got into what is called the "*Devil's Elbow*" and if any place in the wide creation has its own proper name, I thought it was this. Here we had about the hardest work that I ever was engaged in to keep out of danger and even then we were in it all the while. We twice attempted to land at Wood-yards, which we could see, but couldn't reach.

The people would run out with lights and try to instruct us how to get to shore, but all in vain. Our boats were so heavy that we couldn't take them much any way, except the way they wanted to go and just the way the current would carry them. At last we quit trying to land and concluded just to go ahead as well as we could, for we found we couldn't do any better. Some time in the night I was down in the cabin of one of the boats, sitting by the fire, thinking on what a hobble we had got into and how much better bear-hunting was on hard land than floating along on the water, when a fellow had to go ahead whether he was exactly willing or not.

The hatchway into the cabin came slap down, right through the top of the boat, and it was the only way out except a small hole in the side, which we had used for putting our arms through to dip up water before we lashed the boats together.

We were now floating sideways and the boat I was in was the hindmost as we went. All at once I heard the hands begin to run over the top of the boat in great confusion and pull with all their might. The first thing I know'd after this we went broadside full tilt against the head of an island where a large raft of drift timber had lodged. The nature of such a place would be, as everybody knows, to suck the boats down and turn them right under this raft; and the uppermost boat would, of course, be suck'd down and go under first. As soon as we struck, I bulged for my hatchway as the boat was turning under sure enough. But when I got to it, the water was pouring thro' in a current as large as the hole would let it and as strong as the weight of the river could force it. I found I couldn't get out here, for the boat was now turned down in such a way that it was steeper than a house-top. I now thought of the hole in the side, and made my way in a hurry for that. With difficulty I got to it and when I got there, I found it was too small for me to get out by my own dower and I began to think that I was in a worse box than ever. But I put my arms through and hollered as loud as I could roar, as the boat I was in hadn't yet quite filled with water up to my head. The hands who were next to the raft, seeing my arms out and hearing me holler, seized them and began to pull. I told them I was sinking and I pull my arms off, or force me through, for now I know'd well enough it was neck or nothing, come out or sink.

By a violent effort they jerked me through but I was in a pretty pickle when I got through. I had been sitting without any clothing over my shirt; this was torn off; and I was literally skin'd like a rabbit. I was, however, well pleased to get out in any way, even without shirt or hide; as before I could straighten myself on the boat next to the raft, the one they pull'd me out of went entirely under and I have never seen it any more to this day. We all escaped on to the raft, where we were compelled to sit all night about a mile from land on either side. Four of my company were bareheaded and three barefooted; and of that number I was one. I reckon I looked like a pretty cracklin ever to get to Congress!!!

We had now lost all our loading and every particle of our clothing, except what little we had on, but over all this, while I was setting there in the night floating about on the drift, I felt happier and better off than I ever had in my life before, for I had just made such a marvellous escape that I had forgot almost everything else in that; and so I felt prime.

In the morning about sunrise, we saw a boat coming down and we hailed her. They sent a large skiff and took us all on board and carried us down as far as Memphis. Here I met with a friend that I never can forget as long as I am able to go ahead at any thing; it was a Major Winchester, a merchant of that place. He let us all have hats and shoes and some little money to go upon and so we all parted.

A young man and myself concluded to go on down to Natchez to see if we could hear any thing of our boats, for we supposed they would float out from the raft, and keep on down the river. We got on a boat at Memphis, that was going down, and so cut out. Our largest boat, we were informed, had been seen about fifty miles below where we stove and an attempt had been made to land her but without success, as she was as hard-headed as ever.

This was the last of my boats and of my boating, for it went so badly with me, along at the first, that I hadn't much mind to try it any more. I now returned home again and as the next August was the Congressional election, I began to turn my attention a little to that matter, as it was beginning to be talked of a good deal among the people.

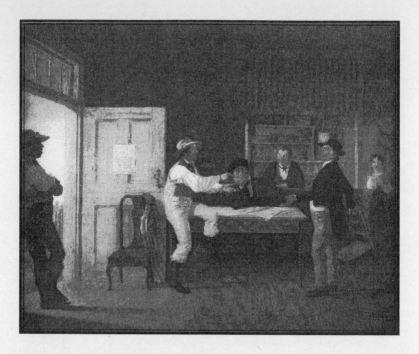

* * *

I HAVE heretofore informed the reader that I had determined to run this race to see what effect the price of cotton could have again on it. I now had Col. Alexander to run against once more and also General William Arnold.

I had difficulties enough to fight against this time, as every one will suppose; for I had no money and a very bad prospect, so far as I know'd, of getting any to help me along. I had, however, a good friend who sent for me to come and see him. I went and he was good enough to offer me same money to help me out. I borrowed as much as I thought I needed at the start and went ahead. My friend also had a good deal of business about over the district at the different courts and if he now and then slip'd in a good word for me, it is nobody's business. We frequently met at different places and, as he thought I needed, he would occasionally hand me a little more cash so I was able to buy a little of "the *creature*" to put my friends in a good humour, as well as the other gentlemen, for they all treat in that country not to get elected, of course; for that would be against the law but just, as I before said, to make themselves and their friends feel their keeping a little.

Nobody ever did know how I got money get along on till after the election was over and I had beat my competitors twenty-seven hundred and forty-eight votes. Even the price of cotton couldn't save my friend Aleck this time. My rich friend, who had been so good to me in the way of money, now sent for me and loaned me a hundred dollars and told me to go ahead; that that amount would bear my expenses to Congress and I must then shift for myself. I came on to Washington and draw'd two hundred and fifty dollars and purchased with it a check on the bank at Nashville and enclosed it to my friend; and I may say, in truth, I sent this money with a mighty good will, for I reckon nobody in this world loves a friend better than me, or remembers a kindness longer.

I have now given the close of the election, but I have skip'd entirely over the canvass, of which I will say a very few things in this place; as I know very well how to tell the truth, but not much about placing them in book order so as to please critics.

Col. Alexander was a very clever fellow and principal surveyor at that time, so much for one of the men I had to run against. My other competition as a major-general in the militia, and an attorney general at the law and quite a smart, clever man also and so it will be seen I had war work as well as law trick to stand up under. Taking both together, they make a pretty considerable of a load for any one man to carry. But for war claims, I consider myself behind no man except "the government" and mighty little, if any, behind him; but this the people will have to determine hereafter, as I reckon it won't do to quit the work of "reform and retrenchment" yet for a spell.

But my two competitors seemed some little afraid of the influence of each other but not to think me in their way at all. They, therefore, were generally working against each other while I was going ahead for myself and mixing among the people in the best way I could. I was as cunning as a little red fox and wouldn't risk my tail in a "committal" trap.

I found the sign was good almost everywhere I went. On one occasion, while we were in the eastern counties of the district, it happened that we all had to make a speech and it fell on me to make the first one. I did so after my manner and it turned pretty much on the old saying, "A short horse is soon curried," as I spoke not very long. Colonel Alexander followed me and then General Arnold come on.

The general took much pains to reply to Alexander but didn't so much as let on that there was any such candidate as myself at all. He had been speaking for a considerable time when a large flock of guinea-fowls came very near to where he was and set up the most unmerciful chattering that ever was heard, for they are a noisy little brute any way. They so confused the general that he made a stop and requested that they might be driven away. I let him finish his speech and then walking up to him, said aloud, "Well, colonel, you are the first man I ever saw that understood the language of fowls." I told him that he had not had the politeness to name me in his speech and that when my little friends, the guinea-fowls, had come up and began to holler "Crockett, Crockett, Crockett," he had been ungenerous enough to stop and drive *them* all away. This raised a universal shout among the people for me and the general seemed mighty bad plagued. But he got more plagued than this at the polls in August, as I have stated before.

This election was in 1827 and, I can say, on my conscience, that I was, without disguise, the friend and supporter of General Jackson upon his principles as he laid them down and as "I understood them" before his election as president. During my two first sessions in Congress, Mr. Adams was president and I worked along with what was called the Jackson party pretty well. I was re-elected to Congress in 1829 by an overwhelming majority and soon after the commencement of this second term, I saw, or thought I did, that it was expected of me that I was to bow to the name of Andrew Jackson and to follow him in all his motions and mindings and

turnings, even at the expense of my conscience and judgment. Such a thing was new to me and a total stranger to my principles. I know'd well enough, though, that if I didn't "hurra" for his name, the hue and cry was to be raised against me and I was to be sacrificed, if possible. His famous, or rather I should say his in-*famous*, Indian bill was brought forward and I opposed it from the purest motives in the world. Several of my colleagues got around me and told me how well they loved me and that I was ruining my self. They said this was a favourite measure of the president and I ought to go for it. I told them I believed it was a wicked, unjust measure and that I should go against it, let the cost to myself be what it might; that I was willing to go with General Jackson in every thing that I believed was honest and right but, further than this, I wouldn't go for him or any other man in the whole creation; that I would sooner be honestly and politically d—nd than hypocritically immortalized. I had been elected by a majority of three thousand five hundred and eighty-five votes and I believed they were honest men and wouldn't want me to vote for any unjust notion to please Jackson or any one else. At any rate, I was of age and was determined to trust them. I voted against this Indian bill and my conscience yet tells me that I gave a good honest vote and one that I believe will not make me ashamed in the day of judgment. I served out my term, and though many amusing things happened, I am not disposed to swell my narrative by inserting them.

When it closed, and I returned home, I found the storm had raised against me sure enough and it was echoed from side to side and from end to end of my district that I had turned against Jackson. This was considered the unpardonable sin. I was hunted down like a wild varment and in this hunt every little newspaper in the district and every little pin-hook lawyer was engaged. Indeed, they were ready to print any and everything that the ingenuity of man could invent against me. Each editor was furnished with the journals of Congress from head-quarters and hunted out every vote I had missed in four sessions, whether from sickness or not, no matter, and each one was charged against me at eight dollars. In all I had missed about seventy votes, which they made amount to five hundred and sixty dollars, and they contended I had swindled the government out of this sum, as I had received my pay, as other members do. I was now again a candidate in 1830 while all the attempts were making against me and every one of these little papers kept up a constant war on me, fighting with every scurrilous report they could catch.

Over all I should have been elected, if it hadn't been, that but a few weeks before the election, the little four-pence-ha'penny limbs of the law fell on a plan to defeat me, which had the desired effect. They agreed to spread out over the district and make appointments for me to speak almost everywhere to clear up the Jackson question. They would give me no notice of these appointments and the people would meet in great crowds to hear what excuse Crockett had to make for quitting Jackson.

But instead of Crockett's being there, this small-fry of lawyers would be there with their saddle-bags full of the little newspapers and their journals of Congress. They would get up and speak and read their scurrilous attacks on me and would then tell the people that I was afraid to attend and in this way would turn many against

me. All this intrigue was kept a profound secret from me till it was too late to counteract it and when the election came, I had a majority in seventeen counties, putting all their votes together, but the eighteenth beat me and so I was left out of Congress during those two years. The people of my district were induced, by these tricks, to take a stay on me for that time but they have since found out that they were imposed on, and on re-considering my case, have reversed that decision which, as the Dutchman said, "is as fair a ding as eber was."

When I last declared myself a candidate, I knew that the district would be divided by the Legislature before the election would come on and I moreover knew that from the geographical situation of the country, the county of Madison, which was very strong and which was the county that had given the majority that had beat me in the former race, should be left off from my district.

But when the Legislature met, as I have been informed, and I have no doubt of the fact Mr. Fitzgerald, my competitor, went up and informed his friends in that body, that if Madison county was left off, he wouldn't run; for "that Crockett could beat Jackson himself in those parts in any way they could fix it."

The liberal Legislature you know, of course, gave him that county and it is too clear to admit of dispute that it was done to make a mash of me. In order to make my district in this way, they had to form the southern district of a string of counties around three sides of mine, or very nearly so. Had my old district been properly divided, it would have made two nice ones in convenient nice form. But as it is, they are certainly the most unreasonably laid off

of any in the state, or perhaps in the nation, or even in the te-total creation.

However, when the election came on, the people of the district, and of Madison county among the rest, seemed disposed to prove to Mr. Fitzgerald and the Jackson Legislature that they were not to be transferred like hogs and horses and cattle in the market and they determined that I shouldn't be broke down, though I had to carry Jackson and the enemies of the bank and the legislative works all at once. I had Mr. Fitzgerald, it is true, for my open competitor but he was helped along by all his little lawyers again, headed by old Black Hawk, as he is sometimes called, (alias) Adam Huntsman, with all his talents for writing *"Chronicles"* and such like foolish stuff.

But one good thing was, and I must record it, the papers in the district were now beginning to say "fair play a little" and they would publish on both sides of the question. The contest was a warm one and the battle well-fought; but I gained the day and the Jackson horse was left a little behind. When the polls were compared, it turned out I had beat Fitz just two hundred and two votes, having made a mash of all their intrigues. After all this, the reader will perceive that I am now here in Congress, this 28th day of January in the year of our Lord one thousand eight hundred and thirty-four and that I am at liberty to vote as my conscience and judgment dictates to be right without the yoke of any party on me or the driver at my heels, with his whip in hand, commanding me to ge-wo-haw just at his pleasure. Look at my arms, you will find no party hand-cuff on them! Look at my neck, you will not find there any collar with the engraving:

MY DOG.

ANDREW JACKSON.

But you will find me standing up to my rack, as the people's faithful representative and the public's most obedient, very humble servant.

DAVID CROCKETT.

PART TWO

An Account of Col. Crockett's
Tour to the North and Down East

AN

ACCOUNT

OF

COL. CROCKETT'S TOUR

TO THE

NORTH AND DOWN EAST,

IN THE YEAR OF OUR LORD ONE THOUSAND
EIGHT HUNDRED AND THIRTY-FOUR.

HIS

OBJECT BEING TO EXAMINE THE GRAND MANUFACTURING ESTABLISHMENT
OF THE COUNTRY; AND ALSO TO FIND OUT THE CONDITION
OF ITS LITERATURE AND MORALS, THE EXTENT OF ITS COMMERCE,
AND THE PRACTICAL OPERATION

OF

"THE EXPERIMENT."

———————

"When thou dont read a book, do not turn the leaves only,
but gather the fruit."

———————

WRITTEN BY HIMSELF.

———————

PHILADELPHIA:
E. L. CAREY AND A. HART.
BALTIMORE:
CAREY, HART & CO.
———————
1835.

Chapter 5
I Tour the East / New York / Boston

During the session of this Congress, I thought I would take a travel through the Northern States. I had braved the lonely forests of the West, I had shouldered the warrior's rifle in the far South; but the North and East I had never seen. I seemed to like members of Congress who came from these parts and wished to know what kind of constituents they had. These considerations, in addition to my physician's advice to travel a little for my health, induced me to leave Washington on the 25th day of April, 1834, and steer for the North.

I arrived the same evening at Barnum's Hotel in Baltimore. Uncle Davy, as he is often called, was right glad to see me, perhaps because we were namesakes or maybe he always likes to see folks patronize his house. He has a pleasant face and his acts don't belie it. No one need look for better quarters; if they do, it will be because they don't know when they are satisfied.

Shortly after I arrived, I was called upon and asked to eat supper with a number of gentlemen. I went and passed the evening pleasantly with my friend Wilkes and others.

Early next morning, I started for Philadelphia, a place where I had never been. I sort of felt lonesome as I went down to the steamboat. The idea of going among a new people, where there are tens of thousands who would pass me by without knowing or caring who I was, who are all taken up with their own pleasures or their own business, made me feel small and, indeed, if any one who reads this book has a grand idea of his own importance, let him go to a big city and he will find that he is not higher valued than a coon-skin.

The steamboat was the Carroll of Carrollton, a fine craft with the rum old commodore Chaytor for head man. A good fellow he is, all sorts of a man, bowing and scraping to the ladies, nodding to the gentlemen, cursing the crew, and his right eye broad-cast upon the "opposition line," all at the same time. "Let go!" said the old one and off we walked in prime style.

We immediately came past Fort McHenry, justly celebrated for its gallant defence under Armistead, Stewart, Nicholson, Newcomb, and others during the last war; and shortly after we passed North Point, where the British landed to make what they never dared, an attack on Baltimore.

Our passage down the Chesapeake bay was very pleasant and in a very short run we came to the place where we were to get on board of the railroad cars.

This was a clean new sight to me; about a dozen big stages hung on to one machine and to start up hill. After a good deal of fuss, we all got seated and moved slowly off, the engine wheezing as if she had the tizzick. By-and-by she began to take short breaths and away we went with a blue streak after us. The whole distance is seventeen miles and it was run in fifty-five minutes.

While I was whizzing along, I burst out a laughing. One of the passengers asked me what it was at. "Why," says I, "it's no wonder the fellow's horses run off." A Carolina wagoner had just crossed the rail-road from Charleston to Augusta when the engine hove in sight with the cars attached. It was growing dark and the sparks were flying in all directions. His horses ran off, broke his wagon and smashed his combustibles into items. He run to a house for help and when they asked him what scared his horses, he said he did not jist know, but it must be hell in harness.

At Delaware City, I again embarked on board of a splendid steamboat, which ran to Philadelphia.

When dinner was ready, I set down with the rest of the passengers; among them was the Rev. O. B. Brown of the Post Office Department, who sat near me. During dinner, the parson called for a bottle of wine and called on me for a toast. Not knowing whether he intended to compliment me or abash me among so many strangers, or have some fun at my expense, I concluded to go ahead and give him and his likes a blizzard. So our glasses being filled, the word went round, "a toast from Colonel Crockett." I gave it as follows: "Here's wishing the bones of tyrant kings may answer in hell, in place of gridirons, to roast the souls of Tories on." At this the parson appeared as if he was stump't. I said, "Never heed; it was meant for where it belonged." He did not repeat his invitation and I ate my dinner quietly.

After dinner I went up on the deck and saw the captain hoisting three flags. Says I, "What does that mean?" He replied that he was under promise to the citizens of Philadelphia, if I was on board, to hoist his flags, as a friend of mine had said he expected I would be along soon.

We went on till we came in sight of the city and as we advanced towards the wharf, I saw the whole face of the earth covered with people, all anxiously looking on towards the boat. The captain and myself were standing on the bow-deck; he pointed his finger at me, and people slung their hats, and huzzaed for Colonel Crockett. It struck me with astonishment to hear a strange people huzzaing for me and made me feel sort of queer. It took me so uncommon unexpected, as I had no idea of attracting attention. But I had to meet it, and so I stepped on to the wharf, where the folks came crowding around me saying, "Give me the hand of an honest man." I did not know what all this meant, but some gentleman took hold of me, and pressing through the crowd, put me into an elegant barouche, drawn by four fine horses; they then told me to bow to the people, I did so and with much difficulty we moved off. The streets were crowded to a great distance and the windows full of people looking out I, supposed, to see the wild man. I thought I had rather be in the wilderness with my gun and dogs than to be attracting all that fuss. I had never seen the like before and did not know exactly what to say or do. After some time we reached the United States Hotel in Chesnut Street.

The crowd had followed me, filling up the street and pressing into the house to shake hands. I was conducted up stairs and walked out on a platform, drew off my hat, and bowed round to the people. They cried out from all quarters, "A speech, a speech, Colonel Crockett."

After the noise had quit, so I could be heard, I said to them the following words:

"GENTLEMEN OF PHILADELPHIA:—My visit to your city is rather accidental. I had no expectation of attracting any uncommon attention. I am traveling for my health without the least wish of exciting the people in such times of high political feeling. I do not wish to encourage it. I am unable at this time to find language suitable to return my gratitude to the citizens of Philadelphia. However, I am almost induced to believe it flattery—perhaps a burlesque. This is new to me, yet I see nothing but friendship in your faces and if your curiosity is to hear the backwoodsman, I will assure you I am illy prepared to address this most enlightened people. However, gentlemen, if this is a curiosity to you, if you will meet me tomorrow at one o'clock, I will endeavor to address you in my plain manner." So I made my obeisance to them and retired into the house.

After night, when I could walk out unknown, I went up street or down, I don't know which, but took good care not to turn any corners, for fear I might get lost. I soon found that the streets were laid off square. This I thought was queer enough for a Quaker city, for they don't generally come up square to nothing; even their coats have a kind of slope, at least so they have cut Mister Penn's coat in the capitol. This may be wrong, too, for I was told that when the man who made him first knocked off "the kivers" of the house where he worked at him, he had cut out Mister Penn with a regular built continental cocked hat on and it was so much laughed at, to see such a hat on a Quaker, that as soon as Congress rose, he cut off his head and worked on a new one with a rale sloped broad brim. Which is the honest George Fox hat? I leave for Philadelphia lawyers and persons to decide.

When I went to my room and got to bed, I could not sleep, thinking over all that passed and my promise also to speak the next day, but at last I composed myself with the reflection that I had got through many a scrape before, so I thought I'd trust again to good luck.

Next morning I had the honor of being called on by some old friends whom I knew at Washington—Judge Baldwin, Judge Hemphill, John Sergeant and others, and I took it right kind in them to do so.

Early after breakfast I was taken to the Water-works where I saw several of the gentlemen managers. This is a grand sight and no wonder the Philadelphians ask every one that comes, "Have you seen the Water-works?" Just think of a few wheels throwing up more water than five hundred thousand people can use: yes, and waste, too; for such scrubbing of steps, and even the very pavements under your feet, I never saw. Indeed, I looked close to see if the house-maids had not web-feet, they walked so well in water and as for a fire, it has no chance at all, they just screw on a long hollow leather with a brass nose on it, dash up stairs, and seem to draw on Noah's flood.

The next place I visited was the Mint. Here I saw them coining gold and silver in abundance, and they were the real "e pluribus unum," not this electioneering trash that they sent out to cheat the poor people telling them they would all be paid in gold and silver, when the poor deceived creatures had nothing coming to them. A chip with a spit on the back of it is as good currency as an eagle, provided you can't get the image of the bird. It's all nonsense. The President, both cabinets and Congress to boot, can't enact poor men into rich. Hard knocks, and plenty of them, can only build up a fellow's self.

I asked if the workmen never stole any of the coin. They said not: they got used to it. Well, I thought that was what my parson would call heterodox doctrine, that the longer a man was in temptation, the more he would not sin. But I let it pass, for I had heard that they had got "new lights" in this city and, of course, new and genuine doctrines—so that the Bible-doxy stood no chance. I could not help, barring the doctrine, giving these honest men great credit; especially when I recollected an old sancti-moniouslyfied fellow who made his negroes whistle while they were picking cherries, for fear they should eat some.

From the Mint I was taken to the Asylum for insane persons, went through different apartments, saw men and women, some quite distracted, others not so bad. This was a very unpleasant sight. I am not able, nor do I wish I was able, to describe it. I felt monstrous solemn and could not help thanking God I was not one of them; and I felt grateful in their stead to that city for caring for those who could not take care of themselves, and feeding them that heeded not the hand and heart that provided for them.

On returning to the hotel, the hour had nearly arrived when I was to visit the Exchange. I asked Colonel Dorrance, the landlord, to go with me. He is a very clever man and made me feel quite at home in his house. Whoever goes there once will go back again. So he agreed and off we started.

I had made set speeches in Congress, especially on my Tennessee land bill, when all my colleagues were against me. I had made stump speeches at home in the face of all the little office yelpers who were opposed to me but, indeed, when I got within sight of the Exchange and saw the streets crowded, I most wished to take back my promise but I was brought up by hearing a youngster say, as I passed by, "Go ahead, Davy Crockett." I said to myself, "I have faced the enemy; these are friends. I have fronted the savage red man of the forest; these are civilized. I'll keep cool and let them have it."

I was conducted to the house of a Mr. Neil where I met several gentlemen and took some refreshment, not passing by a little Dutch courage. Of the latter there was plenty and I observed the man of the house, when he asked me to drink, he didn't stand by to see what I took, but turned away and told me to help myself. That's what I call genteel.

Arrived at the Exchange, I crowded through, went up to the second floor and walked out on the porch, drew off my hat and made my bow; speaking was out of the question, the huzzas for Crockett were so loud and so long.

The time had come when my promise must be kept. There must have been more than five thousand people and they were still gathering from all parts. I spoke for about half an hour.

Three times three cheers closed the concern and I came down to the door, where it appeared as if all the world had a desire to shake hands with me. I stood on the door-step and, as Major Jack Downing said, shook hands as hard as I could spring for near an hour. After this I returned to the hotel and remained until night, when I was asked to visit the theatre in Walnut street. The landlord, Dorrance, and others, were to go with me to see Jim Crow. While we were talking about it, one of them said he could go all over the world "To crow juicy." Some laughed very hearty and others did not. I was among the latter, for I considered it a dry joke, although there was something juicy in it. Some of them said it was Latin and that proved to me the reason why I did not laugh; I was tired of the "old Roman." But these Philadelphians are eternally cutting up jokes on words so I puts a conundrum to them and says I, "Can you tell me why the sacking of Jerusalem was like a cider-mill?" Well, they all were stumped and gave it up. "Because it made the

Jews fly." Seeing them so much pleased with this, says I, "Why is a cow like a razor-grinder?" No one could answer. "Well," says I, "I thought you could find that out, for I don't know myself."

We started for the theatre and found a very full house and Jim a-playing for the dear life. Jim makes as good a nigger as if he was clean black, except the bandy legs.

Everybody seemed pleased, particularly when I laughed. They appeared to act as if I knew exactly when to laugh and then they all followed.

What a pity it is that these theatres are not contrived that everybody could go; but the fact is, backwoodsman as I am, I have heard some things in them that was a leetle too tough for good women and modest men; and that's a great pity, because there are thousands of scenes of real life that might be exhibited, both for amusement and edification, without offending. Folks pretend to say that high people don't mind these things. Well, it may be that they are better acquainted with vice than we plain folks; but I am yet to live and see a woman polished out of the natural feelings, or too high not to do things that ain't quite reputable in those of low degree.

Their fiddling was pretty good, considering every fellow played his own piece; and I would have known more about it, if they had played a tune, but it was all twee-wee-tadlum-tadlum-tum-tum, tadle-leedle-tadle-lee-dle-lee. The "Twenty-second of February" or the "Cuckoo's Nest" would have been a treat.

I do not think, however, from all I saw, that the people enjoyed themselves better than we do at a country frolic, where we dance till daylight and pay off the score by giving one in our turn. It would do you good to see our boys and girls dancing. None of your stradling, mincing, sadying; but a regular sifter, cut-the-buckle, chicken-flutter set-to. It is good wholesome exercise and when one of our boys puts his arm round his partner, it is a good hug and no harm in it.

Next morning I was waited on by some gentlemen who presented me with a seal for my watch-chain, which cost forty dollars. I told them I always accepted a present as a testimony of friendship. The engraving on the stone represents the great match race, two horses in full speed and over them the words "Go ahead." It is the finest seal I ever saw and when I returned to Washington, the members almost used it up, making copies to send all over the country.

I was hardly done making my bow to these gentlemen before Mr. James M. Sanderson informed me that the young Whigs of Philadelphia had a desire to present me with a fine rifle, and had chosen him to have her made agreeable to my wishes. I told him that was an article that I knew somewhat about and gave him the size and weight.

You can't imagine how I was crowded to get through every thing. Colonel Pulaski called to take me in his carriage to the Naval Hospital, where they stow away the old sailors on dry land, and a splendid building it is; all made of marble. I did not like the situation, but I suppose it was the best they could get with so much ground to it.

From there we went to the Navy Yard and examined the largest ship ever made in the United States. She was what they called "in the stocks."

I then surveyed the artillery and the balance of the shipping, not forgetting to pay my respects to the officers of the yard, and then returned home with the colonel, where I was kindly treated, both in eating and drinking and so ended another day.

The next morning the land admiral, Colonel Reeside, asked me to call on him and take a ride. I did so and he carried me out to the rail-road and Schuylkill bridge. I found that the railroad was finished near a hundred miles into the interior of the State and is only one out of many, and yet they make no fuss about it.

We drove in past the Girard school, that old man that gave so many millions to Philadelphia and cut out his kin with a crumb. Well, thinks I, blood is thicker than water and the remembrance of friends better than a big name. I'd have made them all rich and give away the balance. But maybe French people don't think like me. This being my last night in Philadelphia, Dorrance gave me what they call a "pick knick" supper; which means as much as me and all my company could eat and drink and nothing to pay.

I had forgot to say that I had spent part of the evening before this with Colonel Saint.

* * *

NEXT morning, Wednesday the 29th, I was invited by Captain Jenkins of the steamboat New Philadelphia, to go on with him to New York. I accepted his offer and started. I saw nothing very particular along the Delaware river except the place where all the hard stone coal comes to; from the interior of Pennsylvania where, I am told, they have mountains of it. After some time, we got upon a rail-road where they say we run twenty-five miles to the hour. I can only judge of the speed by putting my head out to spit, which

I did and overtook it so quick that it hit me smack in the face. We soon arrived at Amboy and took the water again and soon came in sight of the great city of New York, and a bulger of a place it is. The number of the ships beat me all hollow and looked for all the world like a big clearing in the West with the dead trees all standing.

When we swung round to the wharf, it was covered with people who inquired if I was on board; and when the captain told them I was, they slung their hats and gave three cheers.

Immediately a committee came on board, representing the young Whigs, and informed me they were appointed to wait upon me and invite me to the American Hotel. I accepted their offer and went with them to the hotel where I was friendly received, conducted to a large parlor where I was introduced to a great many gentlemen.

I was invited to visit the new and elegant fire-engine and took some refreshment with the managers and returned in time to visit the Park theatre and see Miss Fanny Kemble play in grand style. The house was better filled and the fixings looked nicer than the one in Philadelphia; but any of them is good enough, if they have such pretty play-actors as Miss Kemble. In fact, she is like a handsome piece of changeable silk; first one color, then another, but always the clean thing.

I returned home, as I am told all great folks do, after the lady actor was done and, sitting with my friends, the cry of "fire, fire," struck my ear. I bounced from my chair and ran for my hat. "Sit down, colonel," said one of the gentlemen, "it's not near us." "A'n't you going to help put it out?" "No," said he, laughing, "we have fire companies here and we leave it to them." Well, to me this seemed queer enough, for at home I would have jumped on the first horse at hand and rode full flight bare-backed to help put out a fire.

I forgot that I was in a city where you may live, as they tell me, years and not know who lives next door to you. Still, I felt curious to see how they managed and Colonel Jackson went with me. As it was late, the engines were only assembling when we got there but when they began to spirt, they put out a four story house that was all in a blaze in less than no time. I asked the colonel where they got so much water from. He said it was raised by the Manhattan Bank out of a charter got by Aaron Burr.

Next morning I was invited by Colonel Mapes to walk down to some of the newspaper offices. I proposed to go to the Courier and Enquirer and Star offices: we did so. I like Webb, for he comes out plump with what he has to say. Mr. Noah has another way of using a fellow up: he holds him uneasy, laughs at him and makes other folks do so; teazes him roasts him, until he don't know what ails him nor what hurt him, but he can't help limping.

We went into Pearl street and I could not help wondering if they had as many boxes and bags and things inside of the houses as they had out. Elegant place for a lame man to walk, for every one is like him; first up, then down-then one side, then another, like a pet in a squirrel box. Shortly we came to the Exchange, the place where the merchants assemble every day at one o'clock, to hear all they can and tell as little as possible and where two lines from a knowing correspondent, prudently used, may make a fortune.

I had not been long here before I was surrounded and called on for a speech. I made many apologies, but none seem'd to hit right and I was so hard pressed that I had no corner to get into so, taking my stand upon the steps above them, I spoke awhile.

I returned to the hotel where I found a great many gentlemen waiting to see the wild man from the far West. After spending some time with them, I was taken to Peak's museum. I shall not attempt to describe the curiosities here; it is above my bend. I could not help, however, thinking what pleasure or curiosity folks could take in sticking up whole rows of little bugs, such like varmints. I saw a boy there that had been born without any hands or arms and he took a pair of scissors in his toes, and cut his name in full and gave it to me. This I called a miracle.

From thence I went to the City Hall and was introduced to the mayor of the city and several of the aldermen. The mayor is a plain, common-sense-looking man. I was told he had been a tanner: and that pleased me, for I thought both him and me had clumb up a long way from where we had started and it is truly said, "Honor and fame from no condition rise." It's the grit of a fellow that makes the man.

On my return, I received an invitation from Colonel Draper to dine with him, informing me also that the rale Major Jack Downing was expected to be there. When the hour arrived, I started to walk there, as it was but a short distance. On my way I saw a white man who was in a great rage, cursing a white man-servant. I stopped and said to him, "Hellow, mister! If you was to talk that way to a white man in my country, he'd give you first rate hell." He looked at me and said nothing but walked off. Sure enough, when I got to Colonel Draper's I was introduced to the major. We sat down to a splendid dinner and amused ourselves with some good jokes. But as this was a private party, I don't think it gentlemanly to tell what was said at this time and especially as this was not the only communication I had with the major. One observation, however, was made by him and I gave him an answer which could not offend anybody. "Colonel," says he, "what d'ye sort o' think about gineral matters and things in purticlur?" Knowing him to be a Yankee, I tried to answer him in his own way. So says I, "Major, the Ginneral's matters are all wrong but some purticklar things are very well such, for instance, as the honor I have in dining with you at Colonel Draper's." "Good," says the major, "and we'll talk about them there matters some other time." "Agreed," says I, "major, always at your sarvice."

I found a large company waiting for me when I got back to the hotel and invitation to sup with the young Whigs. Well now, thinks I, they had better keep some of these things to eat for somebody else, for I'm sure I'm as full as a young cub. But right or wrong, I must go in. There I met the honorable Augustus S. Clayton of Georgia, and was right glad to see him, for I knew I could get him to take some of the speaking off of me. He speaks prime and is always ready and never goes off half-cock.

Upwards of one hundred sat down to supper. They were going to toast me but I told some of them near me to toast Judge Clayton first; that there should be more rejoicing over one that was lost and found again, than over ninety and nine such as me that had never strayed away. They did so and he made a speech that fairly made the tumblers hop. He rowed the Tories up and over Salt River.

Then they toasted me as "the undeviating supporter of the constitution and laws." I made a short speech and concluded with the story of the "Red Cow" which was, that as long as General Jackson went straight, I followed him; but when he began to go this way and that way and every way, I wouldn't go after him like the boy whose master ordered him to plough across the field to the red cow. Well, he began to plough and she began to walk and he ploughed all forenoon after her. So when the master came, he swore at him for going so crooked. "Why, sir," said the boy, "you told me to plough to the red cow and I kept after her but she always kept moving."

Next morning being the first day of May, I went to some of the newspaper offices, read the news, and returned to take a ride with Colonel S. D. Jackson in an elegant barouche. We drove up to the city and took a view of the improvements and beautiful houses in the new part. By the time we returned down Broadway, it seemed to me that the city was flying before some awful calamity. "Why," said I, "Colonel, what under heaven is the matter? Everybody appears to be pitching out their furniture and packing it off." He laughed and said this was the general "moving day." Such a sight nobody ever saw unless it was in this same city. It seemed a kind of frolic, as if they were changing houses just for fun. Every street was crowded with carts, drays, and people. So the world goes. It would take a good deal to get me out of my log-house but here, I understand, many persons "move" every year.

Having alighted and taken some refreshment, I asked Colonel Webb to go with me to the "Five Points," a noted place near the centre of the city. This is the place where Van Buren's warriors came from during the election, when the wild Irish, with their clubs and bludgeons, knocked down every one they could find that would not huzza for Jackson. However, I had a great curiosity to see them and on we went, the major and me, and in the midst of that great city we came to a place where five streets all come together and from this it takes the name of the "Five Points." The buildings are little, old, frame houses and looked like some little country village. The houses all had cellars and as that day was fashionable to move, they were moving too. The streets looked like a clearing in my part of the world, as they were emptying and burning the straw out of their beds. It appeared as if the cellars were jam full of people and such fiddling and dancing nobody ever before saw in this world. I thought they were the true "heaven-borns." Black and white, white and black, all hugemsnug together, happy as lords and ladies, sitting sometimes round in a ring with a jug of liquor between them. I do think I saw more drunken folks, men and women, that day than I ever saw before. This is part of what is called by the Regency the "glorious sixth ward;" the regular Van Buren ground-floor. I thought I would rather risk myself in an Indian fight than venture among these creatures after night. I said to the colonel, "God deliver me from such constituents or from a party supported by such. In my country, when you meet an Irishman, you find a first rate gentleman but these are worse than savages. They are too mean to swab hell's kitchen." He took me to the place where the election was held. It appeared to me that all the place round was made ground and that there was more room in the houses under ground than above and I suppose there must have been a flood of rain during the election, which forced those rats out of their holes. There is more people stowed away together here than any place I ever saw. I heard a story, and it is asserted to be true, that about here, some years ago, a committee visited all the houses to see how they were coming on. One house, that was four stories high and four rooms on a floor, had sixteen families in it and four in the garret, which was divided into four parts by a streak of charcoal. An old lady that was spinning up there was asked how they made out. She said pretty well and that they would be quiet enough if it was not for the old woman in the opposite corner, she took boarders and they often made a noise. I believe it is true. What a miserable place a city is for poor people: they are half starved, poorly clothed and perished for fire. I sometimes wonder they do not clear out to a new country where every skin hangs by its own tail but I suppose they think an hour's indulgence in vice is sweet enough for the bitter of the rest.

Coming home, I took notice that the rear of the City Hall was of brown stone while the front and sides were of white marble. I asked the Colonel why that was so. He said the Poor House stood behind when they built the Hall. That is like many a great man: if he gets a fine breast to his jacket, he will make the back of fustian and like thousands of great people, who think that any thing will do for poor folks to look at or eat or wear. Another thing seemed queer to me and that was a bell hanging outside of the steeple of the Hall: It was so big that they could not get it in and rather than lose the money, they hung it outside, never reflecting that even a backwoodsman must laugh at such a Dutch blunder.

On the same walk I was introduced to the honorable Albert Gallatin. He had an old straw hat in his hand, and like every body else, was "mooving" and said he was sorry not to have more time to be acquainted with me. He pointed to the house he was leaving and said it and several others were to be torn down to build a big tavern. It was a very fine house, fit for any man to live in but in, a few hours I saw men on the top of it and before the next evening the daylight was through it. This tavern is to be near the park and is building by John Jacob Astor. It is to cost seven hundred thousand dollars and covers a whole square. Mr. Astor, I am told, begun business in New York as a dealer in furs and is now worth millions. Lord help the beavers and otters! They must have most got used to being skinned by this time. And what a meeting of friends and kin there must have been in his warehouse. "Farewell," said the otter to the beaver, "I never expect to see you again, my dear old friend." "Never mind, my dear fellow," said the beaver, "don't be too much distressed, we'll soon meet at the hatter's shop."

This day a new flag was to be hoisted down on the Battery and I was invited to attend. The artillery, under command of General Morton, paraded and he invited many of his friends to be present. Among the rest, the mayor, Gideon Lee, was there and he addressed the people. Among other things, he told them that that flag-staff was placed where the old one stood when the British evacuated

New York; that they left the flag flying and greased the pole so that it could not be climbed up but at last a sailor got up and tore it down and hoisted the American flag in its place; and when he came down, the people filled his hat with money.

General Morton is a revolutioner and an officer in the society of old soldiers called the "Cincinnati Society" and wears its badge on his breast. He gave an entertainment to his friends on this occasion; for you must know that nobody thinks any thing well done in this place without eating and drinking over it.

This battery a'n't a place, as its name looks like, for keeping and shooting off cannon. It might have been so, long ago; but it is a beautiful meadow of a place, all measured off, with nice walks of gravel between the grass plats full of big shade-trees and filled with people and a great many children that come there to get the fresh air that comes off the water of the bay. This is a beautiful place and you can see Long Island and Staten Island and many others from it. Here is likewise Castle Garden and the bridge that Van Buren wanted to drown the president off of, when him and Major Jack most fell in. The fact is the plan was well enough but General Jackson did not know of it. It was concluded, you see, that the president should make all his big secretaries and Colonel Reeside go before, and him come after and then slam should go the bridge, with the old fellow on it. But he went foremost and when it fell, they didn't catch any but Governor Cass, secretary of war and he only lost his hat and wig, which they say the porpusses carried off and gave to the sea serpent so that he might be on their side in the next oyster war.

After all this, I went that same day to see my young friend Walden and enjoyed myself with some friends till evening.

When I got back to the hotel, I found the bill for the Bowery theatre and it stated I was to be there. Now I knew I had never given the manager any authority to use my name and I determined not to go. After some time, I was sent for and refused and then the head manager came himself. I told him I did not come for a show; I did not come for the citizens of New York to look at, I come to look at them. However, my friends said it would be a great disappointment and might harm the managers and so I went and was friendly received. I remained a short time and returned. So ended the first day of May, 1834, and I should like to see any body who saw more sights in once waking up. In fact, when I got to bed and begun to think them over, I found it would take me to daylight so I just broke off and went to sleep.

Next morning, Colonel Mapes told me he was requested to invite me to come over to Jersey City to see some shooting with a rifle. In the mean time, I had been very kindly invited by Captain Comstock to go that day, at half-past three o'clock, with him to Boston. I concluded to go, as I might never have another opportunity, and it took only eighteen hours to go there.

I went with the colonel to see little Thawburn's seed store and a great place it is, for he has got all kinds of things there and for fear his bird-seed should not be fresh, he keeps a few hundred birds to eat it up in short order. To prove that his flower-seed is prime, he keeps thousands of little pots growing and mostly gits five times as much for the proof as he does for the seed. He is a little, old, weezened-up man, talks broad Scotch and is as active as a terrier dog.

I now started to Jersey City, where I found a great many gentlemen shooting rifles at the distance of one hundred yards with a rest. One gentleman gave me his gun and asked me to shoot. I raised up, off-hand, and cut within about two inches of the centre. I told him my distance was forty yards, off-hand. He loaded his gun and we walked down to within forty yards, when I fired and was deep in the paper. I shot a second time and did the same. Colonel Mapes then put up a quarter of a dollar in the middle of the black spot and asked me to shoot at it. I told him he had better mark the size of it and put his money in his pocket. He said, "Fire away." I did so, and made slight-of-hand work with his quarter. It was now time to return and prepare for my trip to Boston.

* * *

At three o'clock I left the hotel and went over to where the steamboat lay. When I went on board, the captain showed me into a splendid state-room, which I was to occupy for the voyage. So, when I had made toilet, (as great folks say); that is, combed my hair, and taken a glass of brandy and water, I went on deck. There I saw almost as many people as were when I landed and they kept gathering until the whole ground was covered and when we started, they cheered me for some time and all I could do was to stand and bow to them. This brought me into new trouble; for the passengers found I was on board and came round me so that I missed seeing the city until we got past it.

Soon, however, we came to the place called Hell's Gate; so called, I suppose, because the water boils and foams and bounces about as if it was in a pot. I don't think, however, that this is a good name for it, because we are told in the good book that hell's gate is a mighty slick place and easy to get into. Here I first saw a large square-sailed

British merchant ship, under full sail. She was coming in through the channel and I was glad to see that for when we were voting for an appropriation for a fort to defend this place, I heard it said that no foreign ship ever attempted coming in that way. But these are the kind of arguments used most generally by those who oppose internal improvements, harbors, and they fancy things and speak them for truth.

We went on very pleasantly till night and the captain told me if I would rise at daylight, we would be out of sight of land. So I went to bed and rose as soon as I could see. I walked out on deck, and sure enough, there was no land to be seen. We were coming near Fort Juda, a place where the captain informed me people on board was often very sea-sick. So I set myself down for a case but was disappointed; it was quite calm and a clear fine morning and when the sun rose it came up like a ball of fire out of the water and looked, for all the world, as if it had been made for the first time. We went around Point Juda and kept in sight of land on our left hand. There was very little timber to be seen; the whole country appeared to be laid off in fields, divided by stone fences. These were a great curiosity to me and I could not help thinking that their cattle must be well schooled here; for one of my cows would pitch over a dozen such fences without flirting her tail.

We went by the great fort at the Naraganset bay and landed at Newport for a short time. From thence we took our way again to Providence. There I met a large number of the citizens. They cheered me on my arrival and wanted me to stay and partake of a dinner with them. I declined and took my seat in the fast stage. The driver was ordered to go ahead and sure enough he did. It was forty miles to Boston and we run it down in four hours.

What mighty hard land it is on this road and seems as if the whole face of the earth had been covered over with stones as thick as Kentuck land titles but they have got them strung up into fences, as many as they can, by picking of them off but they won't stay picked, for every time they plough, a new crop comes up.

It was somewhere away long here that the Pilgrims landed at Plymouth and begun to people this part of the world; and a hard time they must have had of it in this barren country. It seems odd that they should come all the way across the sea and not look out for good land. However, I suppose it was all right, or God would have given them better pilots. If they had had fine land, they would not have ventured so much on the ocean and would have had less necessity to work hard and bring up their children to industry and give them such cute teaching as makes them know how to make ducks and drakes of us out yonder when they come among us.

You would be as much struck as I was with the handsome houses and nice farms; but when I came to find all out, I didn't wonder so much. This was Captain A and that B's house; and they made money on sea and spent it on land; that's the truth; for Adam himself could not have made it out of the land. So I found out that the most of them owned a little plantation on shore and the run of the sea to work on besides.

One of the passengers, who came from beyond Boston while we were talking over these things, asked me if I knew Captain Silsbee. I told him no. "I guess you do," says he, "he's our senator in Congress; but to home, we old folks call him captain." I told him, certainly I did, but never knew him by that title. "Well, we know that none on 'em boxed a compass longer nor better, and he made a power of money, and during the last war planked up more gold and silver to lend the government than Benton ever counted."

But I must quit philosophy and tell you where I stopped in Boston—and that was just where any one that has plenty of cash, and plenty of good-will for pleasure, would like—in a clean street, with a tavern on one side and the theatre on the other and both called Tremont. Mr. Boyden did not know me, nor me him; but when I told him my name, where they put it on the bar-book, he treated me like an old friend and continued to do so all the time I was there. He gave me a good room and nice bed; and did not, like many landlords, let a stranger take care of himself, but attended to me the kindest in the world. I had seen a great many fine taverns but take this out and out and Tremont House is a smart chance ahead. It is lately built and has every new arrangement and for a house with a couple of hundred people about it, is the quietest I ever was in. His head man of the gap, in the bar, has eyes all round him and Will Scarlet, as he is called by a friend of mine, has the sound of every bell in the house by heart. When I arrived, I knew no one, but in a short time I made many acquaintances and, indeed, was very kindly treated by every person I met. There is a great deal of friendly feeling with the eastern people and folks need not go out of Boston to find rale hospitality.

Next morning I was invited by Mr. Harding to visit his gallery of paintings, where he had a great many specimens of the fine arts and finally he asked me to sit for him until he could get my likeness, which I did, during my stay, and he has it now, hung up among the rest of the fine arts. From there I went to Faneuil Hall, where General Davis showed me all the accoutrements of war for several companies of infantry and riflemen that was deposited in it. These are in snug rooms on each side of the second story and in the middle is the parade-room, where, summer and winter, the companies meet to drill. This is doing things in true style, that is all for use, and no show about it. So instead of hearing a great fuss with volunteers and drilling and all that wheeling and marching, handle cartridge, eyes right; you see a squad of fine soldiers coming out of this same place and squared up as if they were the rale breed.

General Davis informed me this was the house that was called the "cradle of liberty." I reckon old king George thought they were thundering fine children that was rocked in it, and a good many of them, and that no wonder his red-coats were licked when the children came out with soldier clothes on and muskets in their hands. God grant that the liberty-tree bough on which this cradle rocks may never break.

From here I went to the market, which is a small circumstance ahead of anything I ever saw and just where it should be. Now, in Philadelphia, it looks like a long feeding-trough, stuck up in the middle of the city. And how d'ye think it was done? Why, they put a man of head in, as mayor, who laid all his plans, counted the cost, cyphered out the profits and so forth, and then made one pitch right "ahead" and before the ninnies and scarey folks had half done telling their long stories about the dreadful expense, Mayor Quincy's hammers were keeping time on the big granite stones and the beautiful pillars were rising up as if he had just ordered them. In this market-house everything looks like so many different shops or stores, and you are quite indoors, instead of sellers and buyers both being exposed to wet, heat, and cold. The market appeared to be abundantly supplied but, as I thought, rather dear.

After returning home, I was invited over to Roxborough, where they make the Indian-rubber clothing, and shoes. This is done by dissolving the rubber and putting it on silk and other cloth, which entirely turns the rain and still is pliable and not heavy. The proprietor made me a present of a hunting coat, which I have tried, and would risk my powder under it for forty days and nights. It was a great curiosity to see the young ladies cutting out the clothes and sticking them together with-out sewing them. I went also through the shoe factory where they make shoes in the same way without stitching them. I could not help thinking of the Philadelphia girls, thought they ought to have them, to keep their feet dry.

We often wonder how things are made so cheap among the Yankees. Come here, and you will see women doing men's work and happy and cheerful as the day is long and why not? Is it not much better for themselves and families, instead of sitting up all day busy about nothing? It ain't hard work, neither, and looked as queer to me as it would to one of my countrywomen to see a man milking the cows, as they do here.

After I had seen all that was to be seen here, I was taken to Colonel Perkins' carpet factory. There I saw the widest web I ever saw and they were glossing and stamping it in handsome style. I was quite friendly received by the colonel. He is said to be a very rich man; is quite old, but firm and healthy in appearance and uses his riches in the best possible way: by keeping a great many people busy. And he is not one of those foolish people, neither, that strive all their days to see how rich they can die: for he gives with his hands open. I saw one house in Boston which he gave to keep the blind in and was told it was worth fifty thousand dollars.

What a comfort the old gentleman must have when he looks at his great possessions and is calculating not how much he can hoard up but how much he can give away. God never made such men to be envied or I could begrudge him a few of his blessings from the poor and destitute.

At the invitation of the owners of the Indian-rubber factory, I met a number of the citizens of Roxborough and passed a short time with them very pleasantly.

When I returned to the Tremont, I received an invitation from the young Whigs, to sup with them at eight o'clock. I accepted their invitation and then went over to the Navy Yard at Charlestown. I saw many fine ships and among them was the splendid old Constitution. She was lying in dry dock, and had been new timbered in grand style. The likeness of Andrew Jackson was placed on her for a figure-head. I was asked if it was a good likeness. I said I had never seen him misrepresented but that they had fixed him just where he had fixed himself, that was, before the Constitution.

We then went up to the old battle-ground on Bunker's hill, where they were erecting a monument to those who fell in that day-break battle of our rising glory. I felt as if I wanted to call them up and ask them to tell me how to help to protect the liberty they bought for us with their blood; but as I could not do so, I resolved on that holy ground, as I had done elsewhere, to go for my country, always and everywhere.

When I came back from Bunker's hill, I received about a half a dozen invitations from distinguished citizens of Boston, to dine or sup with them, so that it was impossible to attend to all of them unless I had the digestion of a cassowary. I must here state that the citizens generally of Boston are uncommon kind and civil and if they understand the art of making money they know how to spend it. I was entertained like a prince and could have lived there, I suspect, on the same terms for much longer. They appear to me to live generally in New England more snugly and have more kind feelings to one another and live in more peace and harmony than any people I ever was among. And another good thing: they don't forget one another when they are among strangers; old New England binds them hard together and this gives them, as it ought to do, strength and confidence and influence; and with us in the South Yankee cunning is assuming the true name: Yankee knowledge of business and perseverance in whatever they undertake.

During the afternoon many gentlemen came to see me and we spent our time pleasantly until the time came for me to attend upon the young Whigs. A coach and four fine horses was sent for me. This I considered as too much honor but as I take all things as they come, and everything for the best, I stepped into it and off they whirled with the backwoods hunter. Which way they drove I did not know nor did I care. I knew they would not eat supper till I got there and that they would not serve me as Lafayette was served at a certain place where he was expected to land and dine. The steamboat went wrong and he did not arrive; so they eat their dinners and took out the frolic. About sundown, the boat came up, the orator of the day was called for; he was as blind as a pup; but the moment the old general touched the ground, he put at him with abundance of welcomes and compliments about his heroism until he got up in the pathetics when he said, "Glorious Lafayette, the blood you have shed, and the treasures you expended in defence of the liberties of this country, call for our gratitude. I want words to convey my ideas; in fact, (striking his hand on his belly instead of his heart), I'm too full to proceed." The old gentleman seized his hand, gave it a hearty shake, and so the oration ended.

We came to the appointed place, where I was taken in and introduced to about one hundred young gentlemen, true chips of the old block, ready to be rocked in the old cradle, whether for fight or frolic, war or electioneering. They gave me a hearty welcome and made me feel all as one of themselves. So down we sat to an elegant supper, with the best of wine and the champagne foaming up as if you were supping fog out of speaking-trumpets.

After the cloth was removed and several toasts drank, they toasted me very warmly. I rose and addressed them.

Early next morning I got up and my health being much improved, I felt just like I was in peace with myself and all the world. After breakfast, I took a long walk through the city and passed through the Mall. This is a beautiful green of something like forty acres, I should judge, and looks refreshing in the midst of a city. From the top of the State-house I had a fine view of the city and was quite amused to see the representation of a large codfish hung up in the House of Assembly, or General Court, as they call it, to remind them either that they depended a good deal on it for food or made money by the fisheries. This is quite natural to me, for at home I have on one end of my house the antlers of a noble buck and the heavy paws of a bear.

I did not like the statue of General Washington in the State-house. They have a Roman gown on him and he was an American; this ain't right. They did the thing better at Richmond, in Virginia, where they have him in the old blue and buff. He belonged to this country; heart, soul, and body; and I don't want any other to have any part of him, not even his clothes.

I return the officers in the State-house my thanks for their civility. I can't remember all their names, and therefore I won't name any of them.

When I returned to Tremont house, a gentleman invited me to walk with him to the old State-house. When I reached that I saw a great crowd. General Davis conducted me into the house and we went up stairs, where there was a platform. I drew off my hat and bowed to the people; they immediately cheered me and called for a speech which I had to make.

Here now comes a poser. I was invited to dine out; but if I can mind the gentleman's name I wish I may be shot. He lived near Tremont and I hope, if he has curiosity enough to read this here book, that he will write me a letter so that in my second edition I may give his name as large as life, and I beg him to recollect that it ain't every one that signs a letter that makes himself known. Let him write it plain—none of your hieroglyphics—or I won't put him in.

Some would say that they were mortified that they forgot this gentleman's name. I ain't; I'm sorry; but the truth is, I saw so many folks, and so many new things, that it's no wander I should not mind everything. He was a clever fellow, and I know he will forgive me.

When I went home, there I met a young man that was stone blind. "Well," says you, "that's no new thing." Stop, if you please, that puts me in mind of an old parson and a scolding woman that belonged to his church. She told him, in one of her tantrums, that she could preach as well as he could, and he might select the text. "Well," said the old man, "I'll give you one, and you can study over it. It is better to dwell on the house-top than in a wide house with a brawling woman." "You good-for-nothing, impudent, old— what shall I say? Do you go for to call me a brawling woman?" "Dear mistress," said the good old man, "you'll have to study a while longer, for you come to the application of the text before you discuss the doctrine."

Now it was not that I met a blind boy in Tremont house that was any curiosity, but it was his errand. He inquired of the barkeeper for me, as I was standing by him, and said he was sent by the teacher of the blind to invite me to visit the institution and that he would show me the way.

I was told by the gentlemen present that he could go all over Boston. A gentleman accompanied me and we went on till we came to a fine house where the institution was kept. We went and were introduced to the teacher. He asked me if I wished to hear some of them read. I said I did and he ordered a little girl, perhaps ten or twelve years old, to get her book, asked her to find a certain chapter in the Old Testament, and read it. She took up the book and felt with her fingers until she found it. He then told her to read, and she did so with a clear, distinct voice. This was truly astonishing; but on examining their books I found that the letters were stamped on the under side of the paper, so as to raise them above the surface of the upper side; and such was the keenness of their touch that, by passing the end of the finger over the word, it served them for sight, and they pronounced the word. There was a little boy learning to cipher in the same way. The teacher put several questions to him aloud and, putting his fingers together and working with them for a short time, he answered all the questions correctly.

That kind of education astonished me more than anything I ever saw. There were a great many of them. Some were learning to play on the piano-forte and many of them were busy making pretty little baskets, such as are carried by the ladies.

They asked me if I would like to hear them sing and telling them it would please me very much, a number of them came up, and some had musical instruments: one had a large thing which I never saw before, nor did I ask the name; one had a clarionet, and one had a flute. They played and sung together beautifully and, indeed, I never saw happier people in my life. I remained some time with them going over the establishment. This is the house that I mentioned before was given by Colonel Perkins to the blind. There is not such a grand house owned by any person in Washington. What a satisfaction it must be to this old gentleman and others who have helped these unfortunates to see them surrounded with so many comforts!

GENERAL JACKSON SLAYING THE MANY HEADED MONSTER

CHAPTER 6

New England / My Philadelphia Rifle / Yankee Rum

When I returned, there were some gentlemen that invited me to go to Cambridge, where the big college or university is, where they keep ready-made titles or nicknames to give people. I would not go, for I did not know but they might stick an LL. D. on me before they let me go and I had no idea of changing "Member of the House of Representatives of the United States," for what stands for "lazy lounging dunce," which I am sure my constituents would have translated my new title to be, knowing that I had never taken any degree and did not own to any except a small degree of good sense not to pass for what I was not. I would not go it. There had been one doctor made from Tennessee already and I had no wish to put on the cap and bells. I recollect the story of a would-be-great man who put on his sign after his name, in large capitals, D. Q. M. G., which stood for Deputy Quarter Master General but, which one of his neighbors, to the great diversion of all the rest and to his mortification, translated into "damn'd quick made gentleman." No, indeed, not me; anything you please but Granny Crockett; I leave that for others, I'll throw that in to make chuck full the measure of their country's glory.

I told them I did not go to this branding school; I did not want to be tarred with the same stick; one dignitary was enough from Tennessee, that as far as my learning went, I would stand over it and spell a strive or two with any of them, from *a-b-ab* to *crucifix,* which was where I left off at school.

This day I dined out again but I'm most tired talking of dinners, especially after I have eaten them. I went to the theatre that night. The acting was pretty considerable, considering that one actress who, it was very plain, was either a married woman or "had ought to be," as they say there, was playing in the character of a young lady; and one fellow tried to sing that was not half up to a Mississippi boat horn.

We got a little dry or so and wanted a horn, but this was a temperance house, and there was nothing to treat a friend to that was worth shaking a stick at, so says I, "When there was a famine in the land of Canaan, there was plenty of corn in Egypt; let us go over to the Tremont, Boyden keeps stuff that runs friends together and makes them forget which is which." Over we went and soon forgot all about the theatre.

I had promised next morning to go to Lowell with Mr. Lawrence, Mr. Harding and others, but when I woke up it was pouring down rain so that kept me in the house all day.

I was not idle, for I had a heap of talk with the folks in the house. One gentleman asked me to come and see him, but he gave me so many directions about getting to where he lived that I asked him to write it down and told him if ever he came to my part of the country, I hoped he would call and see me. "Well," said he, "how will I find where you live?" "Why, sir, run down the Mississippi till you come to the Obion river, run a small streak up that, jump ashore anywhere and inquire for me."

Says I to one of them, "Do you believe in the sea-sarpint?" "If I don't, there's no snakes. I believe it to be as much true as there is lie in our deacon when he says his red face ain't made by drinking 'New England.'" "Do you consider him dangerous, or is he peaceable?" "Well, now, to keep the truth, I never saw him, but Capting Hodijah Folger said as how he considered the critter as a sort o' so, and a sort o' not." "Had he a long tail?" "Tail, did you say? You'd a died to hear Didge tell about that verming. Didge said he was like skying a copper—head or tail—but you had to guess which. Ses Didge to me, 'Don't you mind,' ses he, 'that are angel what stood with one leg on the sea, and t'other on the dry land?' I guess I do.' 'Well,' ses he to me, 'that are sarpint's skin was long enough to a queued his hair.'"

I was asked to sup with a Mr. Richards, whom I had seen at Washington. He had a house full of ladies and gentlemen, collected to see me so I was on my manners and I hope they were all as much gratified as I was. We had a fine supper, plenty of conversation and some fun. I don't think the northern ladies talk as much publicly as they do in the south and west. In private conversation they are ready enough.

When I got back, I saw my old cock again. "Well," says I, "what do you think of nullification up here?" "Why, they say, some of them, that it was got and bred by the tariff. Squire Williams, my neighbor, said he didn't think so: it was a kind of come-by-chance, that was too wicked to know its own kin; and he thought it was a very ugly thing." "Well," says I to him, "squire, setting a case as how the Congress of Jacksonmen should pass a law taxing of all the looms and spindles and letting cottons and woolens come in from foreign parts, free of duty. What should we do?" "Why, ask 'em to repeal it." "Suppose they would not do it; and when we were growing poorer and poorer, the tax-gatherer should come to sell you out, stock and fluke." "Why, I'd dispute his authority desperately and if that would not do, I'd fight him, by the blue blazes." "And so would I, but ain't that nullifying, or something mighty like it?" "Why," ses he, "the toe that's tramped on feels most and a man that don't swear had better try a stumpy field with a young yoke of cattle." "Well," ses I, "them there people down there fought desperate in the old war. They whipped Captain Cornwallis and scared Sir Harry Clinton out and out and I reckon then no more nor now they don't like nobody to wrong them out of their rights. But I'm glad it's all over and I tell you what I think; you don't work hard enough in the south and take good care of your grounds and cattle and so on; at least, I hearn Josiah Norton say so when he come home from down to south where he had been pedling a spell. Si ses to me, ses he, 'Please goodness! but that's a poor country down yander; it makes the tears come into the kildear's eyes when they fly over the old fields. Dod drot me, if you can ever get a drink of cider!! They ain't got no apples but little runts of things about as big us your thumb and so sour, that when a pig sticks his tooth into 'em, he lays back his jaw and hollers, you might hear him a mile but it's 'eat, pig, or die' for it's all he's got. And then again they're great for huntin of foxes and if you were to see their hounds! lean, lank, labber-sided pups, that are so poor they have to prop up agin a post-and-rail fence 'fore they can raise a bark at my tin-cart. It's the poorest place was ever made.'" "So," said I, "stranger, you had better come down and judge for yourself, both as to principles and habits. You would be as much pleased, I am sure, as I have been in coming north."

Next morning I rose early and started for Lowell in a fine carriage with three gentlemen who had agreed to accompany me. I had heard so much of this place that I longed to see it, not because I had heard of the "mile of gals" no, I left that for the gallantry of the president who is admitted, on that score, to be abler than myself, but I wanted to see the power of the machinery, wielded by the keenest calculations of human skill. I wanted to see how it was that these northerners could buy our cotton and carry it home,

'Well,' says he, 'Colonel, what do you think of my larder?'—'Fine,' says I,
'let's liquor.'

manufacture it, bring it back and sell it for half nothing and, in the
mean time, be well to live and make money besides.

We stopped at the large stone house at the head of the falls of the
Merrimac river, and having taken a little refreshment, went down
among the factories. The dinner bells were ringing and the folks
pouring out of the houses like bees out of a gum. I looked at them as
they passed, all well dressed, lively and genteel in their appearance,
indeed, the girls looked as if they were coming from a quilting frolic.
We took a turn round, and after dining on a fine salmon, again
returned and entered the factories.

The out-door appearance was fully sustained by the whole of the persons employed in the different rooms. I went in among the young girls and talked with many of them. Not one expressed herself as tired of her employment or oppressed with work; all talked well and looked healthy. Some of them were very handsome and I could not help observing that they kept the prettiest inside and put the homely ones on the outside rows.

I could not help reflecting on the difference of condition between these females, thus employed, and those of other populous countries where the female character is degraded to abject slavery. Here were thousands, useful to others, and enjoying all the blessings of freedom with the prospect before them of future comfort and respectability and however we, who only hear of them, may call their houses workshops and prisons, I assure my neighbors there is every enjoyment of life realized by these persons and there can be but few who are not happy. It cannot be otherwise; respectability depends upon being neighbor-like; here everybody works, and therefore no one is degraded by it; on the contrary, these who don't work are not estimated.

There are more than five thousand females employed in Lowell and when you come to see the amount of labor performed by them, in superintending the different machinery, you will be astonished.

Twelve years ago, the place where Lowell now rises in all its pride was a sheep-pasture. It took its name from Francis C. Lowell, the protector of its manufactories, and was incorporated in 1826, then a mere village. The fall, obtained by a canal from the Merrimac river, is thirty-two feet affording two levels for mills of thirteen and seventeen feet; and the whole waters of the river can be used.

There are about fourteen thousand inhabitants. It contains nine meeting-houses, appropriates seven thousand five hundred dollars for free schools, provides instruction for twelve hundred scholars, daily, and about three thousand annually partake of its benefits. It communicates with Boston by the Middlesex canal, (the first ever made in the United States), and in a short time the railroad to Boston will be completed, affording every facility of intercourse to the seaboard.

This place has grown by and must depend on its manufactures. Its location renders it important, not only to the owners, but to the nation. Its consumption not only employs the thousands of its own population, but many thousands far away from them. It is calculated not only to give individual happiness and prosperity, but to add to our national wealth and independence instead of depending on foreign countries, to have our own material worked up in our own country.

Some of the girls attended three looms and they make from one dollar seventy-five cents to three dollars per week after paying their board. These looms weave fifty-five yards per day so that one person makes one hundred and sixty-five yards per day. Everything moves on like clock-work in all the variety of employments and the whole manufacture appears to be of the very best.

The owner of one of the mills, Mr. Lawrence, presented me with a suit of broadcloth made out of wool bought from Mark Cockral of Mississippi, who sold them about four thousand pounds, and it was as good cloth as the best I ever bought for best imported.

The calico made here is beautiful and of every variety of figure and color. To attempt to give a description of the manner in which it is stamped and colored is far beyond my abilities. One thing I must state that after the web is wove, and before they go further, it is actually passed over a red-hot cylinder to scorch off the furze. The number of different operations is truly astonishing and if one of my country-women had the whole of the persons in her train that helped to make her gown, she should be like a captain on a field muster and yet, when you come to look at the cost, it would take a trunk full of them to find these same people in living for one day.

I never witnessed such a combination of industry and perhaps never will again. I saw the whole process, from the time they put in the raw material until it came out completely finished. In fact, it almost came up to the old story of a fellow walking into a patent machine with a bundle of wool under his arm, and coming out at the other end with a new coat on.

Nothing can be more agreeable than the attention that is paid by every one connected with these establishments. Nothing appears to be kept secret, every process is shown and with great cheerfulness. I regret that more of our southern and western men do not go there, as it would help much to do away with their prejudices against these manufactories.

I met the young gentlemen of Lowell, by their particular request, at supper. About one hundred sat down. Everything was in grand order and went off well. They toasted *me* and I enlightened *them* by a speech as good as I could make and, indeed, I considered them a good set of fellows and as well worth speaking to as any ones I had met with. The old saying, "them that don't work should not eat," don't apply to them, for they are rale workies and know how to act genteel, too; for I assure you I was not more kindly and hospitably and liberally treated any where than just by these same people.

After supper I went to my lodgings for the night. Next morning, I took another range round the town and returned to Boston.

Part of this evening I spent at Lieutenant Governor Armstrong's, where I met a number of ladies and gentlemen. Part of it went off very pleasantly with my worthy landlord in his private rooms and I do him the justice to say that while he supplied his visiters with every thing that was nice, he had also picked out for himself as pretty a little bird as ever fluttered and is in good keeping with everything about the establishment.

Having been invited to the theatre, I went over and sat a short time to be looked at. I was very genteel and quiet and so I suppose I disappointed some of them, who expected to see a half horse half alligator sort of fellow.

This was my last night in Boston and I am sure, if I never see the place again, I never can forget the kind and friendly manner in which I was treated by them. It appeared to me that every body was anxious to serve me and make my time agreeable. And as a proof that comes home, when I called for my bill next morning, I was told there was no charge to be paid by me and that he was very much delighted that I had made his house my home. I forgot to mention that they treated me so in Lowell, but it is true. This was, to me, at all events, proof enough of Yankee liberality and more than they generally get credit for. In fact, from the time I entered New England, I was treated with the greatest friendship and I hope never shall forget it and I wish all who read this book, and who never were there, would take a trip among them. If they don't learn how to make money, they will know how to use it and if they don't learn industry, they will see how comfortable everybody can be that turns his hands to some employment.

Next day the stage called for me at seven o'clock and I took my departure from Boston and went to Providence in Rhode Island. Here I was invited to dine at two of the hotels, but declined both. In fact, I was tired out and wanted a day or two to get rested; and my face being turned towards Washington and my business, I thought I had better go ahead.

We had, from Providence, what they call a pretty considerable of a run, and landed safely in New York, that city of eternal din and confusion.

I spent that evening with some ladies and gentlemen and rode out with ____ ____ in his carriage, faster than I ever was driven by horse power, for twenty-five miles.

Next morning I took my leave of the city of New York and arrived safely in Philadelphia.

Having promised Mr. Hoy of Camden to call and see him on my return, and having fixed the time, I went over accompanied by several gentlemen to the Jersey shore, where there were a great many people waiting to receive me. They gave me the hand of friendship and appeared pleased that I had come over to see them. We proceeded to Mr. Hoy's and then I took a walk around through Camden. On returning to Mr. Hoy's I took some refreshments and was called on for a toast, but begged off, as I expected to be called on for one at dinner.

Some time after this we were asked in to dinner and heard some one say he had lost his pocket-book. And in a few minutes a second cry was raised that another man had lost his pocket-book. I then felt for mine, but I felt in vain; it was gone, with one hundred and sixty-eight dollars in it. I told them there was another gentleman that had his deposits removed and it must be a Jackson man who did it, as it was all on their own plan. But as I was among my friends, I knew I was not just a broke man and therefore I shut pan on the subject and fell to eating my dinner. We had every thing that was good to eat and abundance of fine wine, so we soon forgot the ills of life. After the table was cleared and some toasts drunk, they toasted me in a very handsome manner, complimenting me highly for the course I had taken as a public servant. I returned my gratitude in a speech of about half an hour but which, as is said in certain advertisements, would be too tedious to insert.

After spending a pleasant afternoon, I returned to Philadelphia in the horse-boat; the very one, I suppose, the fellow told of when crossing over. He said they had put in a couple of colts, and being very wild, they pitched ahead, ran off with the boat down the river and never stopped till they came up jam against the breakwater.

Next morning I was invited to go on to Baltimore in the People's Line of steamboats. I accepted the proposal and started in the Ohio steamboat. What is a little remarkable is this: that the rail-road line had always heretofore beat the People's Line until that day, when we passed them, and came into port sometime before them. Whether this was because they had me on board or not, I do not pretend to say. Some said if I could tow a boat up the Mississippi, it was no wonder I could help one along on the Chesapeake bay.

Many of my friends met me on the wharf at Baltimore and escorted me to Barnum's, where there was a great crowd of people. They called on me for a speech. I made a great many apologies but none seemed to fit the right place and I was compelled once more to play the orator. As usual, when there is some speaking going on, there is a good deal of eating and drinking; so I eat and drank generously and retired.

Several friends called on me and requested me to visit Major James P. Heath, member of Congress from Baltimore. I did so and stayed a short time at his house and then returned to uncle Davie's.

Next morning I took the stage for Washington. When I arrived at the capitol, I found nothing new, more than they had just got through the appropriation bill and was taking the vote to postpone Mr. Boone's resolution, setting the day of adjournment. I went in while the clerk was calling the ayes and noes and when he came to my name, and I answered, every one was astonished to find me at my post. "Did not I tell you," said I, "that I would not vote on the appropriation bill, but when you came to any thing else, I was 'Charley on the spot?'" I walked about the house, saw my friends, and sat out the Congress. When the House adjourned for good and all, I started for home by the way of Philadelphia.

* * *

Did you, my good reader, ever witness a breaking up of Congress? If not, you had better come and see for yourself. The first thing that is done is to be sure that Sunday shall be one of the last days. That is because we get paid for Sunday and then, as they generally fix at the end of long sessions, on Monday to break up, a good many can start on Saturday evening or Sunday morning, with two days' extra pay in hand, as they never calculate on much to be done on the last day of the session except to send messages to the senate and president that they are ready to adjourn. We generally lounge or squabble the greater part of the session and crowd into a few days of the last of the term three or four times the business done during as many preceding months. You may therefore guess at the deliberations of Congress, when you can't hear for the soul of you, what's going on, nor no one knows what it is but three or four, and when it's no use to try to know. Woe betide a bill that is opposed! It is laid aside for further time that never comes. This is considered, however, by some of the great men as good legislation; to reject every claim, as if the American people was a herd of scoundrels and every petitioner a cheat and therefore they are doing the country service to reject every thing. Most of these worthies are content to vote no and will not trouble themselves to investigate. I don't know what they are made of, for to me nothing is more delightful than to vote for a claim which, I think, is justly due to make them feel as if the government cared for them and their concerns and would pay what was justly due. What do you think would a petitioner care about going to fight for his country who had been dinging at the doors of Congress, ever since the last war, for some claim or other justly due him, but driven from post to pillar because he does not come within the spirit or letter of some general law or because if you pay him, you must treat others like him? This an't the way with private people; they must pay or be called unjust and be sued into the bargain.

When I arrived in Philadelphia, I put up at the United States where I felt a kind of being at home.

Next morning I was informed that the rifle gun which was to be presented to me by the young men of Philadelphia was finished and would be delivered that evening and that a committee had been appointed to wait on me and conduct me to where I was to receive it. So, accordingly, in the evening the committee came and I walked with them to a room nearly fornent the old statehouse;

it was crowded full and there was a table in the centre with the gun, a tomahawk, and butcher-knife, both of fine razor metal, with all the accoutrements necessary to the gun; the most beautiful I ever saw, or any body else; and I am now happy to add, as good as they are handsome. My friend, John M. Sanderson, Esq., who had the whole management of getting her made, was present and delivered the gun into my hands. Upon receiving her, I addressed the company as follows:

"Gentlemen: I receive this rifle from the young men of Philadelphia as a testimony of friendship, which I hope never to live to forget. This is a favorite article with me and would have been my choice above all presents that could have been selected. I love a good gun, for it makes a man feel independent and prepared either for war or peace.

"This rifle does honor to the gentleman that made it. I must say, long as I have been accustomed to handle a gun, I have never seen anything that could come near a comparison to her in beauty. I cannot think that ever such a rifle was made, either in this, or any other country; and how, gentlemen, to express my gratitude to you for your splendid present, I am at loss. This much, however, I will say: that myself and my sons will not forget you while we use this token of your kindness for our amusement. If it should become necessary to use her in defence of the liberty of our country, in my time, I will do as I have done before and if the struggle should come when I am buried in the dust, I will leave her in the hands of some who will honor your present, in company with your sons, in standing for our country's rights.

"Accept my sincere thanks, therefore, gentlemen, for your valuable present, one of which I will keep as a testimony of your friendship, so long as I am in existence."

I then received the gun and accoutrements and returned to the hotel, where I made an agreement with Mr. Sanderson and Colonel Pulaski, to go with them the next day to Jersey shore, at Camden, and try my gun.

Next morning we went out. I had been long out of practice so that I could not give her a fair trial. I shot tolerable well and was satisfied that when we became better acquainted, the fault would be mine if the varmints did not suffer.

I was invited the next day to go up and spend the day at the Fish House on the Schuylkill, where the fathers of our country, in ancient days, used to assemble and spend the day in taking their recreation and refreshments. It has been a noted place ever since and is as beautiful as you can imagine. It is called the twenty-fifth state. They have regular officers and keep up the old customs with a great deal of formality. We amused ourselves shooting and catching perch. We had a nice refreshment and abundance of the best to drink. Every gentleman took a hand in cooking and the day was truly spent in harmony and peace.

The next morning was the Fourth of July and I had received an invitation, while at Washington, to take dinner in the first district, at the Hermitage with the Whigs, and had accepted the invitation.

At an early hour I was invited to the Musical Fund Hall, where an oration was to be delivered; and went with the honorable Messrs. Webster, Poindexter, Man-gum, Ewing, and Robbins; senators; and Mr. Denny, of the House of Representatives. We were conducted up to a gallery in the first story of an immense building, crowded below to overflowing with ladies and gentlemen.

After the address of the orator, the audience was also addressed by all the senators and I was then called on. "A speech from Colonel Crockett," was the cry all over the house. I was truly embarrassed to succeed so many great men, and where I saw so many ladies; but I found no excuse would do and so spoke.

I then returned to the hotel, where I was waited on in a short time by a committee, with a splendid carriage, and was conveyed to the Hermitage, where I met a large concourse of people, and when it was made known that I had arrived, I was received with loud and repeated cheers and peals of cannon. I was conveyed to a large and cool shade and introduced to a vast number of citizens who all appeared glad to see me. I partook of cool drinks of various kinds and amused myself among the people till near the dinner hour. We were then asked to walk out and take our seats on the stand, where the Declaration of Independence was read and a most appropriate address was delivered by the orator of the day.

I was then called on by the crowd for a speech but dinner was ready and we agreed to postpone further speaking until after dinner.

The dinner, in elegance and variety, did honor to the person who prepared it. After the cloth was removed, and the regular toasts given, I was complimented with a toast.

I rose and requested the company to do me the favor to repair to the stand and I would endeavor to address them from it, as the crowd was so great, it would be impossible for me to make them hear at the table and if I had to speak, I desired to gratify all. When we got out, I found a great many ladies surrounding the stand. I made my way to it among the crowd, who were loudly calling out for my speech, and addressed them.

I then thanked the people for their attention and we repaired to the table, filled our glasses, and drank my toast.

By this time, Mr. Webster, Mr. Robbins, and Mr. Denny arrived, and each were severally toasted, and each made a speech. The whole of the day was delightfully spent, everybody seemed pleased, and I enjoyed myself much.

Shortly after this, the committee returned with me, and we went to the Chesnut street theatre. Here I met a great concourse of people, all in a fine Fourth of July condition. Immediately upon its being announced that I had arrived, I was called on from all quarters for a speech. I rose and made an apology that I was so hoarse, speaking so much, that I could hardly be heard. However, no excuse would be taken, so I was conveyed to the centre of the crowd and made them a short address. They gave me two or three thunders like you hear on the stage and then went on with the show.

I soon left them and returned to the hotel and really was worn out with the scenes of the day, and making three off-hand speeches; and I have often thought since, that nothing could have induced me to have done so, if it had not been in Philadelphia and on the Fourth of July. I was stimulated by being in sight of the old State-house and Independence square, where the fathers of our country met, as it were, with halters on their necks, and subscribed their names to that glorious Declaration of Independence.

Next morning, I was introduced to the great powder-maker, Mr. Dupont, who said to me that he had been examining my fine gun and that he had wished to make me a present of half a dozen canisters of his best sportsman's powder. I thanked him, and he went off and in a short time returned with one dozen, nicely boxed up and directed to me. I then made my arrangements to start the next morning.

While walking about that evening with a friend, we called in at a China importer's store. I was introduced to him and after looking at his splendid collection for some time, he told me he had a wish to present me with a large pitcher. I thought the gentleman was joking at first, but he assured me that if I would accept it, he would pack it up in a box so that it could not break and I could carry it home safely. I thanked him sincerely for his friendship. It was sent to me and I carried it home and gave it to my wife, telling her that when I was away that pitcher should remind her that folks get thirsty and the same spirit which prompted the gentleman to give and should make us use it. I am sorry I forgot his name.

Early next morning I set out for Pittsburg by the fast line and had a very pleasant trip over the mountains. I attracted much attention as I passed through Pennsylvania, where it was known who I was. About the middle of the State I met with an old man in a tavern and asked him who was his representative in Congress. "Why," says he, "Dunlap." I told him that could not be, there was but one of that name in and he was from Tennessee. "Well," says he, "it must be Crawford." No, I told him, there was no Crawford in the House. "Well, hang it, then, it must be George Chambers." "Ah, now you're right; I know him well, he's a good fellow, walks the planks straight. I hope you will re-elect him." "Well, I expect we will. I know nothing against him, only he isn't on our side." "What side are you on?" "Well, I'm for Jackson." "Why," said I, "I thought that was no side at all; he's *on top.*" The old man looked at me right hard. Says I, "Mister, what makes you for Jackson?" "Why," says he, "he licked the British at New Orleans and paid off the national debt." "Mister," says I, "who was the officers and soldiers that fought at New Orleans besides General Jackson?" He said he did not know. "Well," says I, "they ought to have a part of the glory anyhow. Now tell me whose money pays off the national debt?" "Why, I suppose, old Jackson's, as they keep so much talk about it." "Well, now, my good old friend, suppose part of it was yours, and part mine, and part everybody's else; and suppose he would have been broke of his office if he had not paid out what a law of Congress made twenty years ago, provided for paying, what is the glory of the whole of this?" He looked kind of stumped. I bid him good bye and told him that he ought to read both sides.

I arrived in Pittsburg in the night and early in the morning went down to the wharf to inquire for a steamboat. I soon found Captain Stone, who commanded the Hunter. He said he had been waiting a day, thinking that I would like to go with him. That was true and I found him all sorts of a clever man. We were to start at ten o'clock. I returned to the tavern where I had put up and a great many gentlemen called to see me and, among others, Mr. Grant, brother-in-law of Governor Carroll, of Tennessee. He invited me to walk through the city and to visit his house, which I did, and he introduced me to a great many of the citizens. I returned and prepared for a start.

My acquaintance in this place was very limited. I had been there before but my name had not made such a noise then as now.

The marks of industry and enterprise are very visible in Pittsburg. It is a perfect workshop and is increasing every year in extent, beauty and population. The aqueduct, and other splendid works terminating the great canal from Philadelphia, speaks highly for Pennsylvania foresight and perseverance. What signifies the debt incurred by her? But it is no debt, in my mind. It is a noble, imperishing and increasing investment for posterity and they will, to remotest ages, bless the men who have sustained so much abuse by the pack out of office and will consider them as the greatest benefactors of their State and of the nation. I say of the nation, for this canal is a new artery in the body politic, through which the life-blood of its future prosperity and union will flow for ever. Its present facilities have brought a part of the State of Ohio, in point of cost of transportation, within two days' drive with a wagon of the city of Philadelphia, and it will be lower still. Is not this national? In its operation? Who can doubt it?

I had heard it said, particularly in New York, that this same canal never could get along because their great western canal would carry all the produce and merchandize and I took some pains to hear a little about it, and am fully persuaded such is not the fact, and never can be. I was informed that the trade on this Pennsylvania canal was four or five times what it was when the first year ended and in a few years would be a profit to the State and, to me it seems clear that no one south of Pittsburg, in Ohio, and elsewhere, are going to send their merchandize way round by the New York canal and run the risks of the lake when they can put them snug into a boat at Philadelphia and land them safe, without risk, in Pittsburg. I wish I could agree with the Pennsylvanians as well in other respects as I do on internal improvements. What will she not do for her inhabitants in a few years when her twenty odd millions, invested in all her vast and various improvements, shall yield but a moderate profit! Her roads will all be paved, her rivers and creeks made navigable, her schools be free for high and low and her inhabitants free from taxation!!! Reader, these events are sure to come.

And here, let me address a word to my own State. Go on with what little you have begun and never rest until you have opened every facility to every part of our State. Though we are divided into east and west, we are all Tennessee. Give a "long pull, and a strong pull, and a pull altogether" and every difficulty will vanish. Give our inhabitants a chance among the rest of the States and you'll not hear so much of Alabama or Arkansas or Texas.

Well, I've got a long slipe off from my steamboat, the Hunter, and I had better look up the captain. So off I starts, trunk, gun-case, old lady's pitcher and all. "How's the water, Captain Stone?" "Why, colonel, the river is pretty considerable for a run, but the water is as cool as Presbyterian charity and the old Monongahela is a leetle of the remains of what Abigail, the wife of old Nabal, carried as a present to David. Clear off the coal-dust out of your wizzand and give us a yarn about your tower." Why, captain, may I be shot if you mightn't run with this same craft of yours down through and out of Symmes's Lower hole and back again, afore I could get through half what I've seen. I've been clean away amongst the Yankees, where they call your name *Stunn.* "Me, Stunn! Well, it's hard that as slick a fellow as me should go by such nick-names. Livin gingers! What d'ye suppose, colonel, they call me in Orlanes?" "I dare say, some hard name." "Only think of the parly vous; some call me Mr. Peer, and some, by jingo, call me Mr. Peter; and you can't beat it out of them. Only think of Sam Gun, the fireman; he took a spree with some of them Charlies, in Orlanes, and they begun to call him Mounsheer Fusil. Well, Sam bore it a good while but at last he told Joe Head, the engineer, that the first fellow who miscalled his father's name should have a tip of his daddle. 'Good,' says Joe; says he, 'Sam, only take care of their *caniffs,* as how they call them long knives.' Well, it wasn't long before Sam peeled the bark off of a parly's knowledge-box, and so Joe and him had it with a cabin full of them. So Sam he got off to the boat, but the calaboos men got Joe so Joe he sends for me, and when they cum for me, they passed the word that Mr. Tate had sent for me. Well, off I goes to the police, and they axed me if I would go bail for Mounsheer Tate 'No,' says I; 'don't know him.' 'Yes, but you do, captain,' said some one inside and when I went in, who should it be but Joe Head transmogrified into Mounsheer Tate!! Well, we got the matter explained and they all laughed and drunk friends. Well, colonel, here's to you; I'm sure you didn't get anything better anywhere and afore we quit, just tell me, did you see the sea-sarpint?" "Wo, indeed, I did not, although I spoke for him not to morning for Louisville, where I arrived the day after. My friends had provided for me at the Louisville hotel, the finest public house I have been in west of the mountains, I was asked to make a speech to the people next day, which I agreed to, as I had no hope of getting off in a boat for a few days. It was published that I was to speak on the next evening so I was sent for in the morning to visit Jeffersonville Springs in Indiana across the river. I went and found a number of ladies and gentlemen, and after being introduced to the company, I was asked to make a speech to which I had but little objection, as I wished to discuss the question of the President vetoing the Wabash appropriation and yet signing the Van Buren, New York, Hudson river bill. This I did, and the people appeared well pleased. I partook of some of the good things of this life with them, exhorting all Jackson Van Buren men to turn from the evil of their ways and took myself off for the other side of the river.

In the evening I attended at the court-house and met the largest concourse of people that ever has been assembled in Louisville since it has been settled. This I was told by a gentleman who had resided there for upwards of twenty years. The people all appeared to be excited with curiosity or something else. I had no idea of attracting so much attention but there I was in the thick of them. I discovered there were a great many ladies amongst the audience and among them the celebrated Mrs. Drake. A stand had been erected for me in the court-house yard on which I stood and addressed the crowd.

I then returned to the hotel and in a short time a committee of the young men waited on me and invited me to a dinner on Thursday as a testimony in favor of my political course. I gave a conditional acceptance, and no boat arriving, I attended and partook of them with a splendid dinner. I was toasted, and made a speech, complimenting the young men for their zeal in the cause of their country. If I had the powers of General Lafayette, I would have written out all my speeches; but I have not, and therefore omit this one. All passed off pleasantly and next day I took the steamboat Scotland, commanded by Captain Buckner, a gentleman, every inch of him. After a fine run, we arrived at Mills' Point on the twenty-second day of July. Here I once more touched the soil of Tennessee and found my son William waiting to carry me home, which was distant thirty-five miles.

When I landed and took out my fine gun, the folks gathered round me to see the great curiosity. A large fellow stepped up and asked me why all the members did not get such guns given them? I told him I got that gun for being honest, in supporting my country instead of bowing down and worshiping an idol. He looked at me and said that was very strong. "No stronger than true, my friend," said I.

In a short time I set out for my own home: yes, my own home, my own soil, my own humble dwelling, my own family, my own hearts, my ocean of love and affection which neither circumstances nor time can dry up. Here, like the wearied bird, let me settle down for awhile and shut out the world.

In the course of a few days, I determined to try my new gun upon the living subject. I started for a hunt and shortly came across a fine buck. He fell at the distance of one hundred and thirty steps. Not a bad shot, you will say. I say, not a bad gun either. After a little practice with her, she came up to the eye prime and I determined to try her at the first shooting-match for beef.

As this is a novelty to most of my readers, I will endeavor to give a description of this western amusement.

In the latter part of summer our cattle get very fat, as the range is remarkably fine, and some one, desirous of raising money on one of his cattle, advertises that on a particular day, and at a given place, a first-rate beef will be shot for.

When the day comes, every marksman in the neighborhood will meet at the appointed place with his gun. After the company has assembled, a subscription paper is handed round, with the following heading:

"A. B. offers a beef worth twenty dollars to be shot for at twenty-five cents a shot." Then the names are put down by each person, thus:

D. C. puts in four shots, . . .	$1 00
E. F. "eight" . .	2 00
G. H. "two". . . .	0 50

And thus it goes round, until the price is made up.

Two persons are then selected, who have not entered for shots, to act as judges of the match. Every shooter gets a board and makes a cross in the centre of his target. The shot that drives the centre, or comes nearest to it, gets the hide and tallow, which is considered the first choice. The next nearest gets his choice of the hind quarters;

the third gets the other hind quarter; the fourth takes choice of the fore quarters; the fifth the remaining quarter; and the sixth gets the lead in the tree against which we shoot.

The judges stand near the tree, and when a man fires they cry out, "Who shot?" and the shooter gives in his name and so on, till all have shot. The judges then take all the boards and go off by themselves, and decide what quarter each man has won. Sometimes one will get nearly all.

This is one of our homely amusements enjoyed as much by us, and perhaps more, than most of your refined entertainments. Here each man takes a part, if he pleases, and no one is excluded unless his improper conduct renders him unfit as an associate.

* * *

I BEGIN this chapter on the 8th day of July, 1835, at Home,
Weakley county, Tennessee. I have just returned from a two weeks'
electioneering canvass and I have spoken every day to large concourses
of people with my competitor. I have him badly plagued, for he
does not know as much about "the Government," the deposites,
and the Little Flying Dutchman, whose life I wrote, as I can tell the
people, and at times he is as much bothered as a fly in a tar pot to
get out of the mess. A candidate is often stumped in making stump
speeches. His name is Adam Huntsman; he lost a leg in an Indian
fight, they say, during the last war, and the Government run him
on the score of his military services. I tell him in my speech that I
have great hopes of writing one more book, and that shall be the
second fall of Adam, for he is on the Eve of an almighty thrashing.
He relishes the joke about as much as a doctor does his own physic.
I handle the administration without gloves, and I do believe I will

double my competitor, if I have a fair shake, and he does not work like a mole in the dark. Jacksonism is dying here faster than it ever sprung up and I predict that "the Government" will be the most unpopular man, in one year more, that ever had any pretensions to the high place he now fills. Four weeks from to-morrow will end the dispute in our elections, and if old Adam is not beaten out of his hunting shirt, my name isn't Crockett.

While on the subject of election matters, I will just relate a little anecdote about myself which will show the people to the east how we manage these things on the frontiers. It was when I first run for Congress; I was then in favor of the Hero, for he had chalked out his course so sleek in his letter to the Tennessee legislature that, like Sam Patch, says I, "there can be no mistake in him," and so I went ahead. No one dreamt about the monster and the deposites at that time and so, as I afterward found, many, like myself, were taken in by these fair promises, which were worth about as much as a flash in the pan when you have a fair shot at a fat bear.

But I am losing sight of my story. Well, I started off to the Cross Roads dressed in my hunting shirt and my rifle on my shoulder. Many of our constituents had assembled there to get a taste of the quality of the candidates at orating. Job Snelling, a gander-shanked Yankee, who had been caught somewhere about Plymouth Bay and been shipped to the west with a cargo of codfish and rum, erected a large shantee and set up shop for the occasion. A large posse of the voters had assembled before I arrived and my opponent had already made considerable headway with his speechifying and his treating when they spied me about a rifle shot from the camp, sauntering along as if I was not a party in business. "There comes Crockett," cried one. "Let us hear the colonel," cried another and so I mounted the stump that had been cut down for the occasion and began to bushwhack in the most approved style.

I had not been up long before there was such an uproar in the crowd that I could not hear my own voice and some of my constituents let me know that they could not listen to me on such a dry subject as the welfare of the nation until they had something to drink and that I must treat them. Accordingly I jumped down from the rostrum and led the way to the shantee, followed by my constituents shouting, "Huzza for Crockett" and "Crockett for ever!" When we entered the shantee, Job was busy dealing out his rum in a style that showed he was making a good day's work of it, and I called for a quart of the best, but the crooked critur returned no other answer than by pointing to a board over the bar, on which he had chalked in large letters, *"Pay to-day and trust to-morrow."* Now that idea brought me up all standing; it was a sort of cornering in which there was no back out, for ready money in the west, in those times, was the shyest thing in all nature, and it was most particularly shy with me on that occasion.

The voters, seeing my predicament, fell off to the other side and I was left deserted and alone, as the Government will be, when he no longer has any offices to bestow. I saw, as plain as day, that the tide of popular opinion was against me and that unless I got some rum speedily, I should lose my election as sure as there are snakes in Virginny, and it must be done soon or even burnt brandy wouldn't save me. So I walked away from the shantee, but in another guess sort from the way I entered it, for on this occasion I had no train after me and not a voice shouted, "Huzza for Crockett." Popularity sometimes depends on a very small matter indeed; in this particular, it was worth a quart of New England rum and no more.

Well, knowing that a crisis was at hand, I struck into the woods with my rifle on my shoulder, my best friend in time of need, and as good fortune would have it, I had not been out more than a quarter of an hour before I treed a fat coon, and in the pulling of a trigger, he lay dead at the root of the tree. I soon whipped his hairy jacket off his back and again bent my steps towards the shantee and walked up to the bar, but not alone, for this time I had half a dozen of my constituents at my heels. I threw down the coon skin upon the counter and called for a quart and Job, though busy in dealing out rum, forgot to point at his chalked rules and regulations, for he knew that a coon was as good a legal tender for a quart in the west as a New York shilling any day in the year.

My constituents now flocked about me and cried, "Huzza for Crockett," "Crockett for ever," and finding the tide had taken a turn, I told them several yarns to get them in a good humor, and having soon dispatched the value of the coon, I went out and mounted the stump without opposition and a clear majority of the voters followed me to hear what I had to offer for the good of the nation. Before I was half through, one of my constituents moved that they would hear the balance of my speech, after they had washed down the first part with some more of Job Snelling's extract of cornstalk and molassess and the question being put was carried unanimously. It wasn't considered necessary to tell the yeas and nays, so we adjourned to the shantee and on the way I began to reckon that the fate of the nation pretty much depended upon my shooting another coon.

While standing at the bar, feeling sort of bashful while Job's rules and regulations stared me in the face, I cast down my eyes and discovered one end of the coon skin sticking between the logs that supported the bar. Job had slung it there in the hurry of business. I gave it a sort of quick jerk and it followed my hand as natural as if I had been the rightful owner. I slapped it on the counter and Job, little dreaming that he was barking up the wrong tree, shoved along another bottle, which my constituents quickly disposed of with great good humor, for some of them saw the trick, and then we withdrew to the rostrum to discuss the affairs of the nation.

I don't know how it was, but the voters soon became dry again and nothing would do, but we must adjourn to the shantee, and as luck would have it, the coon skin was still sticking between the logs, as if Job had flung it there on purpose to tempt me. I was not slow in raising it to the counter, the rum followed of course, and I wish I may be shot, if I didn't, before the day was over, get ten quarts for the same identical skin and from a fellow, too, who in those parts was considered as sharp as a steel trap and as bright as a pewter button.

This joke secured me my election, for it soon circulated like smoke among my constituents and they allowed, with one accord, that the man who could get the whip hand of Job Snelling in fair trade could outwit Old Nick himself and was the real grit for them in Congress. Job was by no means popular; he boasted of always being wide awake and that any one who could take him in was free to do so, for he came from a stock that sleeping or waking had always one eye open and the other not more than half closed. The whole family were geniuses. His father was the inventor of wooden nutmegs, by which Job said he might have made a fortune if he had only taken out a patent and kept the business in his own hands; his mother, Patience, manufactured the first white oak pumpkin seeds of the mammoth kind and turned a pretty penny the first season and his aunt, Prudence, was the first to discover that corn husks, steeped into tobacco water, would make as handsome Spanish wrappers as ever came from Havana and that oak leaves would answer all the purpose of filling, for no one could discover the difference except the man who smoked them, and then it would be too late to make a stir about it. Job himself bragged of having made some useful discoveries; the most profitable of which was the art of converting mahogany sawdust into cayenne pepper, which he said was a profitable and safe business, for the people have been so long accustomed to having dust thrown in their eyes, that there wasn't much danger of being found out.

The way I got to the blind side of the Yankee merchant was pretty generally known before election day and the result was that my opponent might as well have whistled jigs to a milestone as an attempt to beat up for votes in that district. I beat him out and out, quite back into the old year, and there was scarce enough left of him after the canvass was over to make a small grease spot. He disappeared without even leaving a mark behind and such will be the fate of Adam Huntsman, if there is a fair fight and no gouging.

After the election was over, I sent Snelling the price of the rum but took good care to keep the fact from the knowledge of my constituents. Job refused the money and sent me word that it did him good to be taken in occasionally, as it served to brighten his ideas, but I afterwards learnt when he found out the trick that had been played upon him. He put all the rum I had ordered in his bill against my opponent who, being elated with the speeches he had made on the affairs of the nation, could not descend to examine into the particulars of a bill of a vender of rum in the small way.

Chapter 7
I Have My Say / Texas

August 11, 1835. I am now at home in Weakley county. My canvass is over and the result is known. Contrary to all expectation, I am beaten two hundred and thirty votes, from the best information I can get and, in this instance, I may say, bad is the best. My mantle has fallen upon the shoulders of Adam and I hope he may wear it with becoming dignity and never lose sight of the welfare of the nation for the purpose of elevating a few designing politicians to the head of the heap. The rotten policy pursued by "the Government" cannot last long; it will either work its own downfall or the downfall of the republic soon unless the people tear the seal from their eyes and behold their danger time enough to avert the ruin.

I wish to inform the people of these United States what I had to contend against, trusting that the expose I shall make will be a caution to the people not to repose too much power in the hands of a single man, though he should be "the greatest and the best." I had, as I have already said, Mr. Adam Huntsman for my competitor, aided by the popularity of both Andrew Jackson and Governor Carroll, and the whole strength of the Union Bank of Jackson. I have been told by good men that some of the managers of the bank on the days of the election were heard saying that they would give twenty-five dollars a vote for votes enough to elect Mr. Huntsman. This is a pretty good price for a vote and in ordinary times a round dozen might be got for the money.

I have always believed, since Jackson removed the deposites, that his whole object was to place the treasury where he could use it to influence elections and I do believe he is determined to sacrifice every dollar of the treasury to make the Little Flying Dutchman his successor. If this is not my creed, I wish I may be shot. For fourteen years since I have been a candidate I never saw such means used to defeat any candidate, as were put in practice against me on this occasion. There was a disciplined band of judges and officers to hold the elections at almost every poll. Of late years they begin to find out that there's an advantage in this, even in the west. Some officers held the election, and at the same time had nearly all they were worth bet on the election. Such judges, I should take it, are like the handle of a jug all on one side. I am told it doesn't require much schooling to make the tally list correspond to a notch with the ballot box, provided they who make up the returns have enough loose tickets in their breeches pockets. I have no doubt that I was completely rascalled out of my election and I do regret that duty to myself and to my country compels me to expose such villainy.

Well might Governor Poindexter exclaim: "Ah! my country, what degradation thou hast fallen into!" Andrew Jackson was, during my election canvass, franking the extra Globe with a prospectus in it to every postoffice in this district and upon one occasion he had my mileage and pay as a member drawn up and sent to this district, to one of his minions, to have it published just a few days before the election. This is what I call small potatoes and a few of a hill. He stated that I had charged mileage for one thousand miles and that it was but seven hundred and fifty miles and held out the idea that I had taken pay for the same mileage that Mr. Fitzgerald had taken when it was well known that he charged thirteen hundred miles from here to Washington and he and myself both live in the same county. It is somewhat remarkable how this fact should have escaped the keen eye of "the Government."

The general's pet, Mr. Grundy, charged for one thousand miles from Nashville to Washington, was sanctioned by the Legislature, I suppose because he would huzza! for Jackson and because I think proper to refrain from huzzaing until he goes out of office when I shall give a screamer that will be heard from the Mississippi to the Atlantic or my name's not Crockett—for this reason he came out openly to electioneer against me. I now say that the oldest man living never heard of the President of a great nation to come down to open electioneering for his successor. It is treating the nation as if it was the property of a single individual and he had the right to bequeath it to whom he pleased, the same as a patch of land for which he had the patent. It is plain to be seen that the poor superannuated old man is surrounded by a set of horse leeches who will stick to him while there is a drop of blood to be got and their maws are so capacious that they will never get full enough to drop off. The Land office the Post office and the Treasury itself may all be drained and we shall still find them craving for more. They use him to promote their own private interests and for all his sharp sight, he remains as blind as a dead lion to the jackals

who are tearing him to pieces. In fact, I do believe he is a perfect tool in their hands, ready to be used to answer any purpose to promote either their interest or gratify their ambition.

I came within two hundred and thirty votes of being elected, notwithstanding I had to contend against "the greatest and the best" with the whole power of the Treasury against me. The Little Flying

Dutchman will no doubt calculate upon having a true game cock in Mr. Huntsman, but if he doesn't show them the white feather before the first session is over, I agree never to be set down for a prophet, that's all. I am gratified that I have spoken the truth to the people of my district regardless of consequences. I would not be compelled to bow down to the idol for a seat in Congress during life. I have never known what it was to sacrifice my own judgment to gratify any party and I have no doubt of the time being close at hand when I will be rewarded for letting my tongue speak what my heart thinks. I have suffered myself to be politically sacrificed to save my country from ruin and disgrace and if I am never again elected, I will have the gratification to know that I have done my duty. Thus much I say in relation to the manner in which my downfall was effected and in laying it before the public, "I take the responsibility." I may add in the words of the man in the play, "Crockett's occupation's gone."

Two weeks and more have elapsed since I wrote the foregoing account of my defeat and I confess the thorn still rankles, not so much on my own account as the nation's, for I had set my heart on following up the traveling deposites until they should be fairly gathered to their proper nest, like young chickens, for I am aware of the vermin that are on the constant look out to pounce upon them, like a cock at a blackberry, which they would have done long since, if it had not been for a few such men as Webster, Clay, and myself. It is my parting advice that this matter be attended to without delay, for before long the little chickens will take wing and even the powerful wand of the magician of Kinderhook will be unable to point out the course they have flown.

As my country no longer requires my services, I have made up my mind to go to Texas. My life has been one of danger, toil and privation, but these difficulties I had to encounter at a time when I considered it nothing more than right good sport to surmount them; but now I start anew upon my own hook and God only grant that it may be strong enough to support the weight that may be hung upon it. I have a new row to hoe, a long and rough one, but come what will I'll go ahead.

A few days ago I went to a meeting of my constituents. My appetite for politics was at one time just about as sharp set as a saw mill; but late events have given me something of a surfeit, more than I could well digest; still habit they say is second nature and so I went and gave them a piece of my mind touching "the Government" and the succession, by way of a codicil to what I have often said before.

I told them to keep a sharp lookout for the deposites, for it requires an eye as insinuating as a dissecting knife to see what safety there is in placing one million of the public funds in some little country shaving shop with no more than one hundred thousand dollars capital. This bank, we will just suppose, without being too particular, is in the neighborhood of some of the public lands, where speculators, who have everything to gain and nothing to lose, swarm like crows about carrion. They buy the United States' land upon a large scale, get discounts from the aforesaid shaving shop, which are made upon a large scale also upon the United States' funds, and they pay the whole purchase money with these discounts, and get a clear title to the land so that when the shaving shop comes to make a Flemish account of her transactions, "the Government" will discover that he has not only lost the original deposit but a large portion of the public lands to boot. So much for taking the responsibility.

I told them that they were hurrying along a broad M'Adamized road to make the Little Flying Dutchman the successor, but they would no sooner accomplish that end than they would be obliged to buckle to and drag the Juggernaut through many narrow and winding and out-of-the-way paths to hub deep in the mire. That they reminded me of the Hibernian, who bet a glass of grog with a hod carrier that he could not carry him in his hod up a ladder to the third story of a new building. He seated himself in the hod and the other mounted the ladder with his load upon his shoulder. He ascended to the second story pretty steadily, but as he approached the third his strength failed him, he began to totter, and Pat was so delighted at the prospect of winning his bet that he clapped his hands and shouted, "By the powers, the grog's mine," and he made such a stir in the hod that I wish I may be shot if he didn't win it, but he broke his neck in the fall. And so I told my constituents that they might possibly gain the victory but in doing so, they would ruin their country.

I told them, moreover, of my services, pretty straight up and down, for a man may be allowed to speak on such subjects when others are about to forget them, and I also told them of the manner in which I had been knocked down and dragged out and that I did not consider it a fair fight any how they could fix it. I put the ingredients in the cup pretty strong I tell you, and I concluded my speech by telling them that I was done with politics for the present and that they might all go to hell and I would go to Texas.

When I returned home I felt a sort of cast down at the change that had taken place in my fortunes and sorrow, it is said, will make even an oyster feel poetical. I never tried my hand at that sort of writing, but on this particular occasion such was my state of feeling that I began to fancy myself inspired so I took pen in hand, and as usual, I went ahead. When I had got fairly through, my poetry looked as zigzag as a worm fence; the lines wouldn't tally no how so I showed them to Peleg Longfellow, who has a first rate reputation with us for that sort of writing, having some years ago made a carrier's address for the Nashville Banner, and Peleg lopped off some lines and stretched out others; but I wish I may be shot if I don't rather think he has made it worse than it was when I placed it in his hands. It being my first and, no doubt, last piece of poetry, I will print it in this place, as it will serve to express my feelings on leaving my home, my neighbors and friends and country, for a strange land, as fully as I could in plain prose.

Farewell to the mountains whose mazes to me
Were more beautiful far than Eden could be;
No fruit was forbidden, but Nature had spread
Her bountiful board, and her children were fed.
The hills were our garners—our herds wildly grew,
And Nature was shepherd and husbandman too.
I felt like a monarch, yet thought like a man,

As I thanked the Great Giver, and worshiped his plan.

The home I forsake where my offspring arose;
The graves I forsake where my children repose.
The home I redeemed from the savage and wild:
The home I have loved as a father his child;
The corn that I planted, the fields that I cleared,
The flocks that I raised, and the cabin I reared;
The wife of my bosom—Farewell to ye all!
In the land of the stranger I rise or I fall.

Farewell to my country!—I fought for thee well,
When the savage rushed forth like the demons from hell.
In peace or in war I have stood by thy side—
My country, for thee I have lived—would have died!
But I am cast off—my career now is run
And I wander abroad like the prodigal son—
Where the wild savage roves, and the broad prairies spread,
The fallen—despised—will again go ahead!

Afterword

In August of 1835, Davy learned that he'd been defeated for another term in the House of Representatives. Pretty sore he was. *"I have no doubt that I was completely Raskeled out of my Election."*

The Jackson people—and Tennessee was a Jackson stronghold—had been all strong against him and even his erstwhile friends, the Whigs, their bankers and their lobbyists, who had been happy to use or play him in their struggle with Jackson, had now come on all tepid and were cutting him loose.

Davy was fed up. His political career was a bust. His second book was not selling well. He was in debt and tired and more and more often sick with the old malaria from his time exploring in Alabama after the Creek Indian War days. He no longer lived with his family—hadn't for some time now. He drank too much, too often. The next year he would be fifty.

So on November first, Davy and a few friends lit out for Texas. From Memphis, the *Niles Register* reports his quip: *"They can go to hell and I will go to Texas."*

There are two ways to look at this. You might say, should you be so inclined, that here was Davy running off again. After all, he'd done this before in his boyhood and as a young man. He'd run off from school, from his employer and from his family. He was no sooner married than he ran off to fight in the Indian wars and when his enlistment ended he ran off back home, even though the war continued. Back home for a bit less than a year, Davy just couldn't keep still and again ran off from his family and re-enlisted in Jackson's army. Shortly after returning home that time, it was his wife Polly who, in a manner of speaking, did a runner: she up and died. And all this doesn't even count the times Davy moved his family from place to place or took himself off on long hunting and exploring trips whenever he was feeling pressure at home or in his political life or just whenever the itch come on him. You might say Davy was something of a study in mobility; that he seems to have had a thing for leaving. You might even say this propensity to turn his back and hoof-it out of whatever situation in which he found himself was a well-established trait in his character.

Or more generously, you could say that in America in those days it was possible, even common, for a man to re-invent himself, make a new start in a new place, unburdened by old debts and other ties. All a man had to do was up and go. In the 1830s, Texas was the place to go.

In January we hear from him next. In Texas he signs an oath of allegiance to the "Provisional Government of Texas" and is awarded a grant of land. In February he arrives in San Antonio De Bexar.

It is unclear exactly how or why Davy wound up at the Alamo. His friend Sam Huston, commander of the Texicans, didn't believe the Alamo should or could be held against the army of Santa Anna. But Jim Bowie and William Travis were determined to make a stand there and Davy decides to join them.

Over the years there's been a lot of back and forth as to the exact manner of Davy's death at San Antonio. Some hold he died early on in the battle; others speculate that he died fighting in the last ditch, just as the Texans were finally overwhelmed. Still others assert that he was among the prisoners Santa Anna had executed following the battle.

The only thing about which we can really be sure is that David Crockett was killed by Mexican troops when the Alamo fell in early March 1836.